FOOD & WINE

The 100 Best Recipes

BY THE EDITORS OF *FOOD & WINE*

FOOD & WINE
BOOKS

FOOD & WINE® MAGAZINE
EDITOR IN CHIEF **Hunter Lewis**
EXECUTIVE DIRECTOR, CONTENT STRATEGY **Miles Stiverson**
DEPUTY EDITOR **Melanie Hansche**
EXECUTIVE EDITOR **Karen Shimizu**
EXECUTIVE WINE EDITOR **Ray Isle**
DIGITAL EXECUTIVE EDITOR **Ryan Grim**
MANAGING EDITOR **Caitlin Murphree Miller**

FOOD & EDITORIAL
SENIOR FOOD EDITOR **Mary-Frances Heck**
FOOD EDITOR **Josh Miller**
ASSOCIATE FOOD EDITOR **Kelsey Youngman**
ASSOCIATE RESTAURANT EDITOR **Oset Babur**
ASSISTANT EDITOR **Nina Friend**
BUSINESS MANAGER **Alíce Eldridge Summerville**
WINE INTERN **Caitlin A. Miller**

COPY & RESEARCH
COPY DIRECTOR **Jessica Campbell-Salley**
COPY EDITOR **Erin Clyburn**
ASSOCIATE COPY EDITOR **Winn Duvall**

ART
CREATIVE DIRECTOR **Winslow Taft**
ART FELLOW **Rachel Carney**

PHOTO
PHOTO DIRECTOR **Tori Katherman**
PHOTO EDITOR **Dan Bailey**

PRODUCTION
PRODUCTION DIRECTOR **Liz Rhoades**

DIGITAL
SENIOR ENGAGEMENT EDITOR **Meg Clark**
SENIOR EDITOR **Kat Kinsman**
AUDIENCE ENGAGEMENT EDITOR **Caroline Schnapp**
DIGITAL RESTAURANT EDITOR **Maria Yagoda**
ASSOCIATE NEWS EDITOR **Adam Campbell-Schmitt**
DIGITAL REPORTER **Bridget Hallinan**
DIGITAL PHOTO EDITOR **Sarah Crowder**
DIGITAL OPERATIONS EDITOR **Elsa Säätelä**
ASSOCIATE DIGITAL EDITOR **Megan Soll**

CONTRIBUTORS
CULINARY DIRECTOR AT LARGE **Justin Chapple**

MEREDITH CORPORATION CONSUMER MARKETING
DIRECTOR OF DIRECT MARKETING-BOOKS **Daniel Fagan**
MARKETING OPERATIONS MANAGER **Max Daily**
ASSISTANT MARKETING MANAGER **Kylie Dazzo**
CONTENT MANAGER **Julie Doll**
SENIOR PRODUCTION MANAGER **Al Rodruck**

WATERBURY PUBLICATIONS, INC.
EDITORIAL DIRECTOR **Lisa Kingsley**
CREATIVE DIRECTOR **Ken Carlson**
ASSOCIATE EDITOR **Tricia Bergman**
ASSOCIATE DESIGN DIRECTOR **Doug Samuelson**
PRODUCTION ASSISTANT **Mindy Samuelson**
ASSISTANT EDITOR **Will Bortz**
CONTRIBUTING COPY EDITOR **Peg Smith**
CONTRIBUTING PROOFREADER **Gretchen Kauffman**
CONTRIBUTING INDEXER **Mary Williams**

MEREDITH NATIONAL MEDIA GROUP
PRESIDENT AND CEO **Tom Harty**

MEREDITH CORPORATION
EXECUTIVE CHAIRMAN **Stephen M. Lacy**
IN MEMORIAM **E.T. Meredith III (1933–2003)**

CONTENTS

Fish & Shellfish

Pasta &Grains

Desserts

Pork Loin Braised with
Mushrooms, page 132

FOREWORD

IN THE SEPTEMBER 2018 ISSUE OF *FOOD & WINE*, we celebrated our 40th anniversary with a rundown of the 40 best recipes that had appeared on the pages of the magazine since its founding in 1978—one from each issue—along with a little background on the chef, cookbook author, culinary writer, or *F&W* staffer who contributed it.

As we put that special edition together, we reviewed thousands of recipes. We found ourselves asking, "What makes a good recipe?" and "What makes a 'best' recipe?" again and again. The good ones yield a delicious result, of course. The best ones have an additional quality such as timelessness, authenticity, innovation, or simplicity. Or a story to tell.

The process made us want to give *F&W* readers an even more expansive taste of what those four decades had to offer. The result of that is this book. Every recipe in it was chosen not only because it is delicious but also because it has some other compelling quality.

Julia's Favorite Roast Chicken (page 147) is a decidedly unfussy French-style chicken stuffed with sautéed vegetables, lemon, and herbs that is so classic and perfect it is impervious to trends. For chef André Soltner, his mother's Potato and Egg Pie with Bacon and Crème Fraîche (page 85) hearkens to his home in Alsace. Paula Wolfert noted that as he prepared it, there was "pleasure and nostalgia ... plainly on his face." From food-truck pioneer Roy Choi come Kogi Dogs (page 117)—smoky hot dogs piled high with cabbage, kimchi, and cheddar that became a cult favorite on the streets of Los Angeles very shortly after he started serving them in 2008. Catalan Tomato Bread (page 24) from cookbook author Steven Raichlen is the essence of simplicity—grilled country-style bread rubbed with garlic and ripe tomato, drizzled with extra-virgin olive oil, and sprinkled with sea salt and freshly ground black pepper. And Fried Chicken with Tomato Gravy and The Best Biscuits (page 158) from Scott Peacock and Edna Lewis tells a story of Southern heritage but also of a deep and enduring friendship.

As a collection, the recipes in this book document four decades of culinary trends and tastemakers. Although they represent the different roles food plays in our lives—from the need for a quick weeknight dinner to the pleasures of devoting an entire weekend to cook just one amazing dish—there is one constant: Great food makes life better.

Hunter

HUNTER LEWIS
@NOTESFROMACOOK
HUNTER@FOODANDWINE.COM

Zuni Roast Chicken and
Bread Salad, page 161

KNIVES

JAPANESE CHEF'S KNIFE
A basic 8-inch Japanese chef's knife with dimples can be used for most chopping and slicing tasks. (The air in the dimples acts as a nonstick coating between the knife and the food.) It should feel lightweight and balanced in your hands so it's easy to control. This type of knife may be less suited to cutting up a whole chicken than a heavier German knife, but it has just enough heft to get most jobs done.

CLASSIC CHEF'S KNIFE   It doesn't get more essential than this. A heavy 8-inch chef's knife may be less nimble than the Japanese knives we use, but it's powerful, which means it's excellent for butchering and for cubing dense vegetables.

HEAVY-DUTY JAPANESE CHEF'S KNIFE   This knife borrows from ancient Japanese sword-making traditions. It may be a bit of a splurge, but well worth the investment. The blade of more than 70 layers of high-carbon stainless steel is exceptionally sharp, and it stays that way for a very long time. Our honing steel and sharpening stone are starting to collect dust.

PARING KNIVES   Every station in our Test Kitchen has multiple paring knives because they are employed in so many food-prep tasks that require dexterity and precision, like peeling fruit, removing skin from a baked potato, or chopping shallots and garlic.

SERRATED KNIFE   While this may be the least-used knife in the kitchen, it is essential for certain tasks. A sturdy 8-inch slant-tip serrated knife is our tool of choice for cutting crusty loaves and perfectly neat slices of tomatoes for piled-high BLTs.

Classic
chef's knife

Paring knife

Japanese
chef's knife

Heavy-duty Japanese
chef's knife

COOKWARE

ROASTING PANS Whether you're preparing a showstopping holiday roast or a weeknight meal, look for a sturdy roasting pan that can withstand high heat for stovetop searing and sauce-making, even gas grilling. You don't have to spend a fortune. We use a 16-inch stainless-steel roaster that costs less than $50 for most tasks. If you use your pan for more than the occasional roast, look for a larger pan with a 3-inch depth and a flared lip. The flared lip helps with consistent heat circulation, and the wide handles make it easy to hoist in and out of the oven—even when it's holding a 25-pound bird.

POTS & PANS You don't need a set of 20 pans, just five essentials: an oven-safe 12-inch fry pan; a 12-inch nonstick fry pan; 1.5- and 3-quart saucepans; and a 6-quart stockpot. We have dozens of pans, but the ones we reach for over and over are sturdy stainless steel. They heat evenly, go from stovetop to the oven, and are easy to clean and maintain.

DUTCH OVEN A heavy 7-quart Dutch oven made of enameled cast iron is enormously versatile and ticks all our boxes. It heats evenly, is stovetop- and oven-safe and chip-resistant, and has high sides—so it's as ideal for a big batch of soup as it is for frying chicken.

NONSTICK PANS

While a nonstick surface is not ideal for creating a perfectly caramelized crust on a seared steak, every kitchen should be equipped with at least one good-quality nonstick pan. They are essential for cooking eggs—which stick terribly to other materials—and for cooking delicate fish fillets. Look for heavy pans that are oven-safe.

HAND MIXERS

While stand mixers are crucial for some tasks, they are by necessity heavy and unwieldy. Sometimes you just need to whip some cream or whip up some cake batter. We like a hand mixer that has 145 watts of power, 9 speeds for versatility—so it will go low enough to fold flour in without having it fly out of the bowl and all over the kitchen, and a smooth keypad so there's no cleaning between buttons.

MIXERS & BLENDERS

STAND MIXER A quality stand mixer is going to be an investment—upwards of $350 to $400. But you should not skimp. For plowing through a dense cookie dough or kneading stiff bread dough, you want a powerful workhorse whose engine is up to the task. Our stand mixers get a workout. We use them for making everything from dough to meringue and, with some of our favorite attachments, for rolling out pasta, grinding meat, and stuffing sausages.

HIGH-POWERED BLENDER This is another high-ticket expenditure, but a blender with a strong motor and sharp blades is indispensable not only for your morning smoothie but also for making the smoothest soups, creamiest nut butters, and crushed ice for cocktails.

GRINDER Sometimes simple is just better. We love a single-button grinder. We always have two on hand— one for coffee and another for spices like coriander and cumin. Pro tip: Run rice through it to clean and prevent flavor buildup.

GRATERS

BOX GRATER The broad work surface and large sharp holes can quickly shred cheddar cheese and firm vegetables like cabbage and carrots. A less obvious use is pureeing corn kernels from a shucked ear and squishy vegetables like tomatoes (leaving the thin skin behind).

COARSE MICROPLANE This handy little grater has small sharp slits that cut in both directions, making it excellent for thinly shaving chocolate or cheese. A coarse Microplane is also good for making bread crumbs to top grilled vegetables or steaming bowls of pasta.

MICROPLANE Its tiny, ultrasharp holes famously allow the Microplane to scrape zest from citrus without cutting into the pith beneath. The Microplane can also quickly puree small, soft aromatics like garlic and ginger or grate whole spices like cinnamon sticks and nutmeg.

Box grater

Coarse Microplane

Microplane

PAIRING CHEAT SHEET

There's no magic to pairing food with the right wine—just a few simple principles. Here's how to match what you eat to the world's most important wines.

MALBEC   Malbec, Shiraz, and Côtes du Rhône are big and bold enough to drink with foods brushed with robustly spiced barbecue sauces.

SYRAH   When a meat is heavily seasoned, look for a red wine with lots of spicy notes. Syrah from Washington state, Cabernet Franc from France, and Xinomavro from Greece are all good choices.

CABERNET SAUVIGNON   California Cabernet, Bordeaux, and Bordeaux-style blends are terrific with steaks or chops: Their firm tannins refresh the palate after each bite of meat.

ZINFANDEL   If you can use the same adjectives to describe a wine and a dish, the pairing will often work. For instance, the words "rustic" and "rich" describe Zinfandel, Italy's Nero d'Avola, and Spain's Monastrell as well as chicken-liver mousse.

PINOT NOIR   Recipes with ingredients like truffles and other mushrooms taste great with reds like Pinot Noir and Dolcetto, which are light-bodied and full of savory depth.

OLD WORLD WINES   The flavors of foods and wines that have grown up together over the centuries—Tuscan recipes and Tuscan wines, for instance—are almost always a natural fit.

DRY ROSÉ   Some cheeses go better with white wine, some with red; yet almost all pair well with dry rosé, which has the acidity of white wine and the fruit character of red.

ROSÉ CHAMPAGNE   Rosé sparkling wines, such as rosé Champagne, cava, and sparkling wine from California, have the depth of flavor and richness to go with a wide range of main courses.

CHAMPAGNE   Most dry sparkling wines, such as brut Champagne and Spanish cava, have a faint touch of sweetness, which is extra-refreshing served with salty foods.

SAUVIGNON BLANC   Tangy foods won't overwhelm zippy wines like Sauvignon Blanc, Vinho Verde from Portugal, and Verdejo from Spain.

GRÜNER VELTLINER   Austrian Grüner Veltliner's citrus-and-clover scent is lovely with dishes with lots of fresh herbs. Other go-to grapes in a similar style include Albariño from Spain and Vermentino from Italy.

PINOT GRIGIO   Light seafood dishes seem to take on more flavor when matched with equally delicate white wines, such as Pinot Grigio or Arneis from Italy or Chablis from France.

CHARDONNAY   Silky whites—for instance, Chardonnays from California, Chile, or Australia—are delicious with fish like salmon or any seafood in a lush sauce.

OFF-DRY RIESLING   The slight sweetness of many Rieslings, Gewürztraminers, and Vouvrays helps tame the heat of spicy Asian and Indian dishes.

MOSCATO D'ASTI   Moderately sweet sparkling wines such as Moscato d'Asti, demi-sec Champagne, and Asti Spumante emphasize the fruit in the dessert rather than the sugar.

Appetizers & Breads

TIKI SNACK MIX

As the modern craft cocktail movement picked up steam in the early 2000s, tiki cocktails were especially popular, and it seemed only fitting that there should be the perfect cocktail mix to snack on while downing a mai tai or a Singapore Sling. Former *F&W* senior associate recipe developer Melissa Rubel Jacobson put together this irresistible mix of soy-and-honey-glazed peanuts, bacon, and chewy pineapple–combining Polynesian flavors in every bite. The mix complements just about any drink. It's the go-to snack mix for *F&W* parties.

ACTIVE 20 MIN; TOTAL 1 HR 15 MIN; MAKES 4½ CUPS

8 thick-cut bacon slices

3 cups salted roasted peanuts

4 candied pineapple rings, cut into ⅓-inch wedges

2 Tbsp. sesame seeds

1 Tbsp. low-sodium soy sauce

1 Tbsp. honey

¼ tsp. cayenne pepper

Kosher salt

1 Preheat oven to 350°F. Arrange bacon in a single layer on a wire rack set inside a large rimmed baking sheet. Bake in preheated oven until crisp, about 30 minutes. Drain on paper towels, and cut into ½-inch pieces.

2 Toss together bacon, peanuts, pineapple, sesame seeds, soy sauce, honey, and cayenne in a medium bowl. Spread on a rimmed baking sheet and bake at 350°F until bacon is browned, about 20 minutes, stirring once after 10 minutes. Sprinkle with salt, and let stand, stirring occasionally, until cool. —*Melissa Rubel Jacobson*

CORN HUSK GRILLED
GOAT CHEESE WITH HONEY

The balance of flavors and textures in this dish from Portland-based cookbook author Andrea Slonecker is pure genius. With the smoky essence of the husk infused into the hot molten cheese, a generous drizzle of honey melting in, and that charred sweet corn relish-all spooned onto a hunk of crusty bread-plus a bottle of pink bubbly (high in acid to stand up to the tartness of the dish), a patio, and a pile of friends, it's the perfect predinner snack for a summer party.

TOTAL 35 MIN; SERVES 4

- 2 large ears fresh yellow corn
- 1 (8-oz.) goat cheese log, cut in half crosswise, at room temperature, divided
- 2 scallions, white and light green parts only, thinly sliced
- 1 red Fresno chile or red jalapeño, stemmed, seeded, and finely chopped
- 4 tsp. extra-virgin olive oil
- 1 Tbsp. fresh lime juice
- 1 tsp. kosher salt
  Pinch of black pepper
- 3 Tbsp. torn fresh basil
- 3 Tbsp. coarsely chopped fresh cilantro
- 2 Tbsp. honey
  Grilled crostini, for serving

1 Open bottom and top vents of a charcoal grill completely. Light a charcoal chimney starter filled with briquettes. When briquettes are covered with gray ash, pour onto bottom grate of grill and push to one side. Adjust vents as needed to maintain an internal temperature of about 500°F. (If using a gas grill, preheat to very high [about 500°F] on one side.)

2 Working with 1 ear of corn at a time, carefully remove husk, making sure not to tear husk. Remove and discard silk from corn and set corn aside. Overlap a few long edges of husk pieces on a work surface; place 1 goat cheese half lengthwise in center. Continue overlapping remaining husk pieces, cupping them around goat cheese to completely enclose log. (You are essentially replacing the corn cob with the cheese log.) Gather excess husk pieces at each end, and tie with kitchen twine or a piece of corn husk, securing cheese in a cylindrical packet.

3 Stir together scallions, chile, oil, lime juice, salt, and pepper in a medium bowl; set aside.

4 Place goat cheese packets and ears of corn on oiled grates over lit side of grill; grill, covered, turning goat cheese packets and corn often, until packets are charred and cheese is softened, about 4 minutes. Transfer packets to unlit side of grill to keep warm. Continue grilling corn, covered, turning often, until charred in spots and tender, 10 to 12 minutes.

5 Place grilled corn on a cutting board. Using a clean kitchen towel or pair of tongs to stand ears upright, cut kernels from cobs. Add corn kernels, basil, and cilantro to scallion mixture, then toss to combine.

6 Place cheese packets on a serving platter. Cut a slit lengthwise through top layer of charred husks to expose goat cheese. Drizzle cheese with honey, and spoon corn relish over top. Serve hot with grilled crostini. —*Andrea Slonecker*

MAKE AHEAD Recipe may be prepared through Step 3, covered, and chilled until ready to grill, up to 1 day.

WINE Pair with a strawberry-scented sparkling rosé.

ASIAN TUNA TARTARE

While tuna tartare has been a smashing success on restaurant menus, it wasn't so common to make at home, mostly because readers feared working with raw tuna. To ensure that we gave readers the single best recipe, we turned to French chef Eric Ripert–master of all things seafood–for this spot-on dish.

ACTIVE 20 MIN; TOTAL 2 HR 20 MIN; SERVES 4

¼ cup corn oil

2 tsp. grated peeled fresh ginger

1 lb. sushi-grade tuna, cut into ⅛-inch dice

¼ cup finely chopped fresh cilantro, divided

1 tsp. minced jalapeño

1½ tsp. wasabi powder

1 tsp. toasted sesame seeds

1 Tbsp. finely chopped scallion

1½ Tbsp. fresh lemon juice, plus half a lemon

Sea salt

Freshly ground black pepper

1 tomato, peeled, seeded, and cut into ⅛-inch dice

20 best-quality potato chips

1 Combine oil and ginger in a bowl, and let stand at room temperature for at least 2 hours. Pour oil through a fine wire-mesh strainer into a bowl; discard solids.

2 Combine tuna, 3 tablespoons ginger oil, 3 tablespoons cilantro, jalapeño, wasabi, sesame seeds, scallion, and lemon juice in a large bowl. Mix gently, and season with salt and pepper.

3 Stand a 1½-inch-tall and 2¼-inch-round mold or a biscuit cutter in the center of a salad plate. Fill mold with tuna tartare, pressing gently. Lift off mold. Repeat with remaining tartare.

4 Drizzle remaining ginger oil around each tartare, and sprinkle with tomato, remaining 1 tablespoon cilantro, and a squeeze of lemon juice. Stand 5 potato chips in a circular pattern in each tartare and serve immediately. *—Eric Ripert*

CATALAN TOMATO BREAD

The simple act of cutting a tomato and rubbing it on bread creates a magical bite. *Pa amb tomàquet*, a specialty of Barcelona that cookbook author Steven Raichlen shared, offers irrefutable proof that the best dishes are often the simplest. Assemble it in the kitchen, or provide your guests with garlic cloves, halved tomatoes, a cruet of oil, and a bowl of salt and let them do the work. Like all simple dishes, this appetizer from Barcelona's Los Caracoles restaurant demands flawless ingredients: crusty country-style bread; soft, ripe tomatoes; and fragrant olive oil.

TOTAL 15 MIN; SERVES 8

8 (½-inch-thick) slices country-style bread

4 garlic cloves, cut in half (optional)

4 very ripe tomatoes, cut in half

Extra-virgin olive oil (preferably Spanish), for serving

Coarse sea salt

Freshly ground black pepper (optional)

1 Preheat grill to medium-high (about 450°F). Place bread slices on oiled grates; grill, uncovered, until crisp and nicely browned, 2 to 4 minutes per side.

2 Rub one bread slice with the cut side of one garlic half, if using, and the cut side of one tomato half. Repeat procedure with remaining bread slices, garlic halves, and tomato halves. Drizzle each slice with oil, sprinkle with salt and pepper, if using, and eat at once. —*Steven Raichlen*

NOTE In lieu of grilling, bread may be toasted with a toaster.

WINE Pair with a lively dry Cava.

SUMMER VEGETABLE TOWER

The key to this impressive tower from Emily Fiffer and Heather Sperling of Los Angeles' veggie-forward restaurant, Botanica, is to season the vegetables before they go on the platter. "We want all the vegetables to be delicious on their own before they take a dunk in any dip or sauce," says Fiffer. Try tossing some of the veggies with olive oil and seasoning with salt, za'atar, lemon zest, or smoked paprika, like we do here. The vibrant purple dip is a take on muhammara, the Middle Eastern red pepper spread. "I love the texture and sweet earthiness that comes from the raw beet," she says. We do too.

TOTAL 45 MIN; SERVES 8 TO 10

1 lb. small potatoes

Kosher salt and black pepper

1 Tbsp. plus 2 tsp. extra-virgin olive oil, plus more for brushing

¼ tsp. smoked paprika

8 oz. multicolor carrots, sliced ½ inch thick on the bias

Green Tahini (recipe follows), for serving

Beet Muhammara (recipe follows), for serving

Grilled ciabatta bread, sliced vegetables—such as radishes with greens, pattypan squash, thinly sliced fennel, sliced Persian cucumbers, endive spears, Romanesco and/or cauliflower florets, blanched Broccolini, and blanched green and/or wax beans— for serving

Edible flowers and herb sprigs (optional), for garnish

1 In a large pot, cover the potatoes with cold water and bring to a boil. Add a generous pinch of salt and simmer until tender, 15 to 20 minutes. Drain and let cool, then halve the potatoes.

2 Light a grill and oil the grate. In a medium bowl, toss the potatoes with 1 tablespoon of the olive oil and ⅛ teaspoon of the paprika. Season with salt and pepper. Grill the potatoes, turning, until lightly charred, about 6 minutes. Transfer to a plate and let cool completely. Keep the grill on.

3 Meanwhile, in a medium bowl, toss the carrots with the remaining 2 teaspoons of olive oil and ⅛ teaspoon of paprika. Season with salt and pepper. Grill the carrots, turning once, until tender and lightly charred, about 6 minutes. Transfer to a plate and let cool completely.

4 Set the tahini and muhammara on a large platter or tiered stand. Arrange the grilled bread and the blanched, grilled, and raw vegetables in bunches around the dips. Garnish with edible flowers and herb sprigs; serve. —*Emily Fiffer & Heather Sperling*

GREEN TAHINI In a blender, puree ¾ cup chopped dill sprigs, ½ cup tahini, ½ cup fresh lime juice (from 4 limes), 2 tablespoons extra-virgin olive oil, 1 teaspoon finely chopped garlic, 1 teaspoon vadouvan (see Note*) until smooth. With the machine on, drizzle in ⅓ cup warm water until incorporated. If the dip is too thick, add more water, 1 tablespoon at a time. Season generously with kosher salt. Transfer to a small bowl.

BEET MUHAMMARA In a small skillet, toast 1½ tsp. ground cumin over moderately high heat until fragrant, 1 minute. Transfer to a food processor. Add 1 large peeled and chopped red beet, ¾ cup chopped toasted walnuts, 3 tablespoons fresh lemon juice, 1 tablespoon pomegranate molasses, 1 garlic clove, and 1¼ teaspoons Urfa biber (see Note**). Pulse to finely chop. With the machine on, drizzle in ¼ cup extra-virgin olive oil until the dip is almost smooth. Season with kosher salt. Transfer to a small bowl and garnish with more walnuts and Urfa.

NOTE* Vadouvan, a French spice blend inspired by Indian curry, is available at Whole Foods and from amazon.com.

NOTE** Urfa biber, or Urfa pepper, is a smoky, sour Turkish chile. It's available at laboiteny.com or amazon.com.

GEORGIAN HOMESTYLE CHEESE BREAD (KHACHAPURI)

Though Georgian food and khachapuri have been getting a lot of attention recently, this was a pretty unknown region of the world (not to mention the recipe) in 1990, when the remarkable Paula Wolfert taught **F&W** readers all about the cuisine and shared this extraordinary bread baked with cheese. We fell in love.

ACTIVE 1 HR 20 MIN; TOTAL 2 HR 20 MIN; MAKES TWO 7-INCH ROUND BREADS

2 cups unbleached all-purpose flour (9 oz.), divided, plus more for dusting

3 Tbsp. sunflower oil or canola oil

¾ cup plain yogurt

1 Tbsp. cornstarch

¾ tsp. baking soda

¼ tsp. kosher salt

½ cup feta cheese (2 oz.) or ¼ cup crumbled Roquefort cheese (1 oz.)

1 cup grated fresh mozzarella (4 oz.)

1 small egg, beaten

1 tsp. unsalted butter, melted

1 Combine ⅓ cup flour and oil in a medium bowl and blend. Add yogurt and, mixing thoroughly, stir in another ⅓ cup flour. Sift together cornstarch, baking soda, and salt; stir into flour mixture. Gradually add enough remaining flour to form a soft, but not sticky, dough. Lightly dust dough with flour, cover with a kitchen towel, and set aside in a warm place to rest for 1 to 2 hours.

2 If using feta cheese, soak cheese in water for 10 minutes, then drain well and crumble. Using a fork, mix feta and mozzarella with egg in a medium bowl, and shape into two even balls. Set aside.

3 Divide dough into two portions and roll into balls. Keep one ball covered while shaping the other. On a floured surface, flatten ball of dough into a 7-inch round. Generously dust your hands and the dough with flour. Gently rotate and pull the piece of dough into an even 10-inch circle, about ¼ inch thick. Be careful not to tear the dough.

4 Pat one ball of cheese mixture into a 5-inch circle in center of dough. Gently pull edge of dough up over filling, pleating and pinching to seal. Pat into a 7-inch round.

5 Heat a large, well-seasoned cast-iron or nonstick skillet over low for 3 minutes. Lightly film the skillet with some of the melted butter, then slide bread, seam side up, into skillet. Cover and cook, shaking pan occasionally, for 12 minutes.

6 Uncover and flip bread; cover and continue cooking over low, shaking skillet occasionally, until bread is deep golden brown, about 12 minutes. Lightly brush top with butter, and slide bread onto a wooden board. Let stand 5 minutes. Repeat with remaining dough and cheese filling. Use a serrated knife to cut into wedges. Serve warm. —*Paula Wolfert*

PAULA WOLFERT

Paula Wolfert wrote for *F&W* for 35 years, from its founding in 1978 until 2013, when she retired from teaching and writing after a diagnosis of dementia. The duration may seem unusual because she explored ancient ways of cooking with the same passion *F&W* scouts new ones. But Wolfert was always making new discoveries about those old ways. In her articles, as in her nine seminal Mediterranean cookbooks—including books on the foods of Morocco, southwest France, and the eastern Mediterranean—she explains obscure ingredients and complex techniques with enthusiasm and rigor. America's embrace of Mediterranean foods was due in large part to her almost anthropological approach to food.

She won the Julia Child Award three times, the James Beard Award five times, the M.F.K. Fisher Award, and the Tastemaker Award.

In 2008, Emily Kaiser Thelin, a former *F&W* staffer and author of *Unforgettable: The Bold Flavors of Paula Wolfert's Renegade Life* (2017), traveled to Marrakech with Wolfert. "As she quizzed a sausage vendor about his grilling technique, I worried he'd get annoyed," Thelin wrote in a 2013 issue of *F&W*. "But like the rest of us, he warmed immediately to this exuberant woman with her insatiable curiosity about food."

Wolfert brought a maternal warmth to her relentless questioning and could charm almost anyone into sharing their food knowledge—and we're all better off for it.

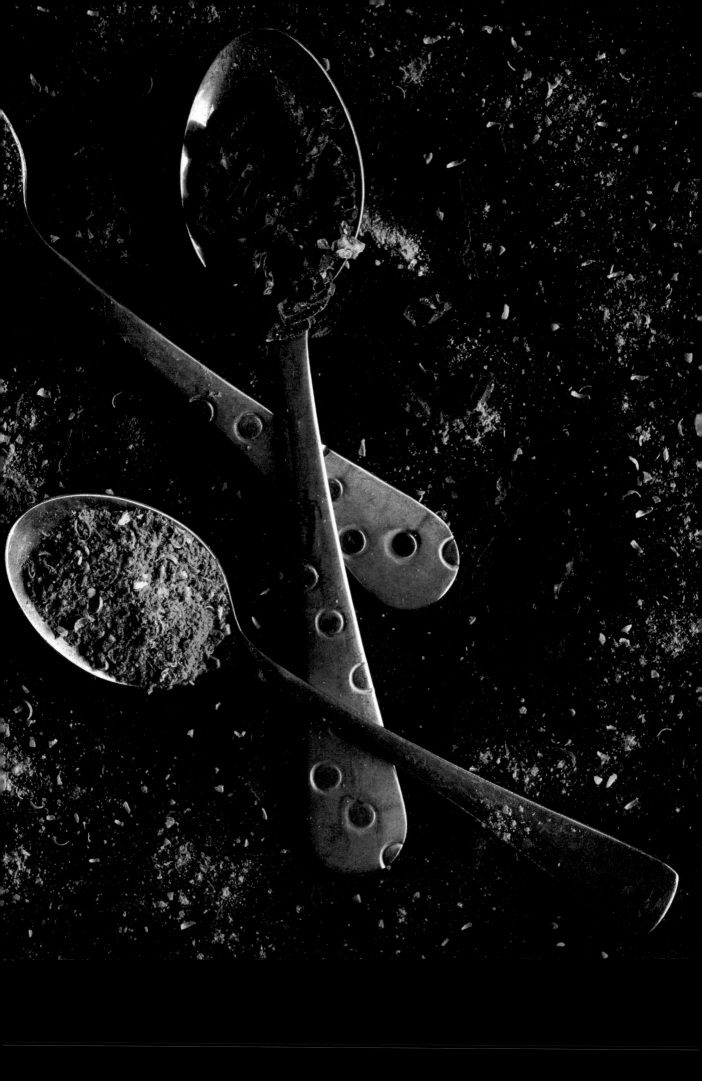

ANGEL BISCUITS

These biscuits are the lightest and most buttery ones we've ever tried. They come from Scott Howell, the chef/owner of Nana's in Durham, North Carolina, who shared his family recipe in the April 2001 issue of *F&W*. Also called bride's biscuits, these are popular with novice cooks because the two leaveners make the recipe virtually foolproof. The dough needs to be refrigerated overnight, so plan accordingly.

ACTIVE 30 MIN; TOTAL 2 HR 30 MIN, PLUS OVERNIGHT CHILLING; MAKES 40 BISCUITS

2¼ tsp. active dry yeast (about 1 [⅛-oz.] envelope)

¼ cup plus pinch of granulated sugar

2 Tbsp. lukewarm water

5 cups self-rising flour (about 20 oz.), plus more

1 cup cold solid vegetable shortening, cut into small pieces

2 cups buttermilk

6 Tbsp. unsalted butter, melted

1 Dissolve yeast and a pinch of sugar in lukewarm water in a small bowl and let stand until foamy, for 5 minutes. Mix flour with remaining ¼ cup sugar in a large bowl. Using a pastry blender, or your fingers, work shortening into flour until mixture resembles very coarse crumbs with some pieces the size of small peas. Add yeast mixture and buttermilk, then stir until dough just comes together.

2 Turn dough out onto a lightly floured work surface, and knead 5 times; the dough should be soft and moist. Transfer dough to a clean bowl; cover with plastic wrap and refrigerate overnight.

3 Transfer dough to a lightly floured surface, and knead 10 times. Roll out or pat dough to a 16-inch round ⅓ inch thick. Using a 2¼-inch biscuit cutter, stamp out biscuits as close together as possible. Pat dough scraps together, reroll, and cut out remaining biscuits (do not overwork dough). Discard any remaining scraps.

4 Lightly butter 2 large baking sheets. Brush tops of biscuits with melted butter. Fold biscuits in half, brush tops with remaining melted butter, and set them, unbuttered side down, on prepared baking sheets. Cover loosely with plastic wrap and let rise in a draft-free place for 2 hours.

5 Preheat oven to 400°F. Bake biscuits about 15 minutes, or until browned on bottom and light golden on top. Serve warm. —*Scott Howell*

MAKE AHEAD The dough can be prepared through Step 2 and refrigerated up to 2 days.

MISO BANANA BREAD

The miso in this supremely delicious banana bread adds deep, robust flavor. Though the two James Beard-winning Bostonian chefs, Jamie Bissonnette and Ken Oringer, think the bread is fantastic the day it's made, they say it tastes even better the following day.

ACTIVE 30 MIN; TOTAL 2 HR; MAKES ONE 10-BY-5-INCH LOAF

5 medium overripe bananas

1¾ cups all-purpose flour (about 7¾ oz.)

1 tsp. baking soda

½ tsp. baking powder

¼ tsp. kosher salt

½ cup unsalted butter (4. oz), softened

1 cup granulated sugar

¼ cup white miso

½ cup buttermilk

2 large eggs

1 Preheat oven to 350°. Butter and flour a 10- x 5-inch metal loaf pan. Using a fork, mash 4 of the bananas in a large bowl until chunky. Whisk the flour, baking soda, baking powder, and salt in another bowl.

2 Cream the butter, sugar, and miso with a stand mixer fitted with the paddle at medium speed until fluffy, about 5 minutes. Reduce to low speed, slowly add the buttermilk, then beat in the eggs 1 at a time until incorporated. Beat in the mashed bananas; the batter will look curdled. Add the flour mixture, and mix until just blended. Scrape into prepared pan.

3 Slice remaining banana lengthwise and arrange banana halves on top of the batter side by side, cut side up. Bake in preheated oven until a wooden pick inserted in center comes out clean, 90 minutes. Place bread on wire rack for 30 minutes before turning out to cool completely. —*Jamie Bissonnette and Ken Oringer*

MAKE AHEAD. The banana bread can be wrapped in plastic and kept at room temperature up to 3 days.

Soups

FRESH PEA SOUP WITH HAM

This crazy-smart twist on pea soup from Chicago chef Graham Elliot floored us. The anise flavor of the fennel pairs perfectly with the sweetness of the peas—and the spoonful of ham salad adds a touch of smoke and salt. Sometimes you don't think a classic dish needs any kind of reinvention, but this was so delicate and satisfying that it convinced us all to make pea soup in summer.

TOTAL 45 MIN; SERVES 4

- 1 Tbsp. unsalted butter
- 1 small fennel bulb, thick stalk discarded, bulb thinly sliced
- ½ medium onion, thinly sliced
- 2 garlic cloves, chopped
  Kosher salt
- 1 qt. whole milk
- 4 cups fresh or frozen peas (1 lb.), thawed
- ½ cup diced smoked ham hock (from one 11-oz. ham hock) or smoky ham
- 1 Tbsp. minced shallot
- ½ Tbsp. chopped chives
- 1 tsp. extra-virgin olive oil
- ½ tsp. sherry vinegar
  Pea tendrils or baby arugula, for garnish

1. Melt butter in a large saucepan over medium. Add fennel, onion, and garlic, and season with salt. Cook, stirring, until vegetables are tender but not browned, 8 to 10 minutes. Add milk and simmer for 15 minutes. Add peas and simmer until tender, 7 to 8 minutes.

2. Working in batches, puree soup in a blender. Pour liquid through a fine wire-mesh strainer into a large bowl. Season with salt.

3. Combine ham, shallot, chives, oil, and vinegar in a small bowl. Spoon ham salad into centers of 4 bowls. Ladle warm soup into bowls, garnish with pea tendrils, and serve immediately. —Graham Elliot

POSOLE ROJO

Food writer Priya Krishna describes posole as "the choose-your-own-adventure" of Mexican cuisine. You start with a stew speckled with chewy bits of hominy and seasoned with lime and braised pork. Depending on the region, that soup could be green from jalapeños and tomatillos (if you're in Guerrero) or red from guajillo or ancho chiles (in Mexico City and Jalisco). Then, choose from a selection of toppings: chopped onions, sliced avocado, lime, radishes, lettuce, queso fresco. Go big, or keep it simple. That's the true beauty of posole: No two bowls look or taste exactly alike.

ACTIVE 2 HR 10 MIN; TOTAL 5 HR 25 MIN; SERVES 10

- 1 (3-lb.) boneless pork shoulder (Boston butt), trimmed and cut into 2-inch pieces
- 1 (3-lb.) rack pork spareribs, cut in half crosswise
- 6 qt. water, plus more
- 2 Tbsp. plus 2 tsp. kosher salt, divided
- 1 large white onion, quartered
- 3 large garlic cloves
- 1 (2-inch) piece fresh ginger, peeled
- 3 bay leaves
- 1 Tbsp. dried oregano, plus more for serving
- 3 (25-oz.) cans white hominy, drained and rinsed (about 8 cups)
- 5 large dried ancho chiles, split, stems and seeds discarded
- 5 large dried guajillo chiles, split, stems and seeds discarded
- 2 Tbsp. grapeseed oil
- 10 (5-inch) corn tostada shells
- 4 cups thinly sliced iceberg lettuce (from ½ head lettuce)
- 3 cups chicharrones (optional)
- 1 cup crumbled Cotija cheese (optional)
- 8 red radishes, thinly sliced
- 2 ripe medium-size avocados, thinly sliced
- 5 limes, halved

1. Combine pork shoulder, spareribs, 6 quarts water, and 1 tablespoon salt in a large stockpot. Bring to a boil over high, skimming off and discarding foam from surface during first 10 minutes of cooking. Place onion, garlic, ginger, bay leaves, and oregano in center of a large piece of cheesecloth; gather edges of cheesecloth together, and secure with twine. Add to pot; reduce heat to medium-low, and gently simmer, uncovered, 1 hour and 30 minutes.

2. Remove cheesecloth bundle from pot. Remove onion, garlic, and ginger; set aside. Discard bay leaves and oregano. Add hominy to pot; simmer over medium-low, uncovered, until rib bones can be easily removed from spareribs, about 1 hour and 30 minutes.

3. Meanwhile, place half the chile halves in a large, deep skillet over medium. Cook, turning occasionally, until toasted evenly on both sides, about 1 minute. Transfer to a plate; repeat with remaining chiles. Return all toasted chiles to skillet; add water to cover. Bring to a simmer over medium; cook until chiles are soft and rehydrated, about 15 minutes. Remove from heat; cool for 15 minutes. Drain chiles; taste cooking liquid. If it tastes bitter, discard. If it tastes faintly of raisins, reserve ½ cup.

4. Transfer chiles and either reserved ½ cup cooking liquid or ½ cup water to a blender. Add onion, garlic, ginger, and 1 tablespoon salt. Process until smooth, adding splashes of stock from pork mixture, about 1 minute. Pour through a fine wire-mesh strainer into a bowl; discard solids.

5. Heat oil in a 10-inch skillet over medium-high. Once hot, add chile mixture. Cook, stirring often, until reduced by half and darkened in color, about 30 minutes. Remove from heat, and set aside.

6. Remove spareribs from stockpot, and set aside; let cool for about 5 minutes. Discard rib bones and tendons from spareribs. Chop meat into bite-size pieces, and return to stockpot. Stir in reserved chile sauce. Bring to a simmer over medium-low; cook until flavors meld, about 1 hour, skimming fat from surface, if desired. Stir in remaining 2 teaspoons salt.

7. To serve, place tostada shells; lettuce; chicharrones, if using; Cotija, if using; radishes; avocados; and limes in separate bowls. Ladle soup evenly among 10 large bowls. Sprinkle with oregano. Serve soup alongside bowls of garnishes for diners to customize their servings. —*Priya Krishna*

MAKE AHEAD Prepare soup through Step 6; cool soup, cover, and chill up to 3 days. Prepare garnishes for Step 7 just before serving. Rewarm soup gently before serving with garnishes.

NOTE Soaking dried chiles draws out their flavor, including bitterness, if prevalent. If the resulting liquid is sweet, incorporate it into the dish. Discard it if it tastes bitter.

CHICKEN PHO

Because pho is largely about the flavor of the broth, using a high-quality bird here is key. Jimmy Tu of Manhattan's Bunker gently poaches the chicken until it's cooked just enough so he can remove the meat from the bones and shred it. Then he returns the skin and bones to the pot to simmer for a few more hours.

ACTIVE 20 MIN; TOTAL 6 HR 30 MIN; SERVES 8

PHO

- 1 Tbsp. kosher salt, plus more to taste
- 1 (3½-lb.) whole chicken
- 2 whole star anise
- 2 cardamom pods
- 1 tsp. coriander seeds
- 1 2½-inch cinnamon stick
- 1 tsp. black peppercorns
- ½ tsp. white peppercorns
- 1 tsp. goji berries
- 2 shallots, halved
- 1 small onion, quartered
- 1 leek, halved lengthwise and cut into 2-inch pieces
- 1 Tbsp. crushed rock sugar or dark brown sugar
- 1 Tbsp. Asian fish sauce

GARNISHES

- ¼ cup canola oil
- 3 medium shallots, thinly sliced (1 cup)
- 6 oz. dried rice noodles
- ¼ cup sliced scallions
- ¼ cup chopped fresh cilantro
   Bean sprouts, basil sprigs, mint sprigs, thinly sliced jalapeños, and lime wedges, for serving

1 MAKE THE PHO Bring 5 quarts of water to a boil in a large stockpot. Add 1 table-spoon of salt and the chicken, breast side down. Place a heatproof plate over chicken to keep it submerged and bring to a boil. Reduce heat and simmer 30 minutes; it will not be cooked through. Transfer chicken to a bowl of ice water, and let cool completely. Drain well and pat dry.

2 Meanwhile, combine the star anise, cardamom, coriander, cinnamon stick, black and white peppercorns, and goji berries in a large cast-iron skillet. Cook over medium-low, stirring, until very fragrant, about 3 minutes. Transfer to a small bowl. In the same skillet, combine shallots, onion, and leek. Cook over medium, stirring occasionally, until deep golden, about 10 minutes.

3 Remove meat from chicken, and coarsely shred it. Return all the chicken skin and bones to the broth in the stockpot. Add the pan-roasted shallot, onion, and leek mixture, and bring to a boil. Cover and simmer over moderately low heat for 1 hour. Stir the toasted spices and goji berries into the broth. Cover and simmer for 1 hour longer. Add rock sugar and simmer for another 30 minutes. Strain broth into a large bowl, pressing on solids; discard solids. Pour the broth into a clean saucepan.

4 MAKE THE GARNISHES Heat oil in a large skillet over medium. Add shallots and cook, stirring frequently, until golden brown, 5 to 7 minutes. Using a mesh skim-mer, transfer the shallots to a paper-towel-lined plate to drain. Let cool. Cook rice noodles in a large pot of boiling water until pliable, 8 to 10 minutes.

5 Bring pho broth to a simmer. Stir in shredded chicken, and cook until just white throughout, 1 to 2 minutes. Stir in fish sauce, and season broth with salt. Drain rice noodles, and transfer to large bowls.

6 Ladle broth and chicken over noodles. Top with scallions and cilantro. Garnish with crispy shallots, bean sprouts, basil, mint, and jalapeños. Serve with lime wedges. —*Jimmy Tu*

MAKE AHEAD The poached chicken and finished broth can be refrigerated separately overnight.

WINE Fragrant Northern Italian white, such as a Pinot Bianco.

BURMESE SAMUSA SOUP

This vegan soup from Desmond Tan's Burma Superstar in San Francisco is the restaurant's most popular soup for meat eaters and vegetarians alike. It features a broth that's seasoned with black mustard seeds, cumin, and turmeric. Fresh cabbage, herbs, and chiles top each ample bowl, contrasting tender lentils and potatoes with a pleasing crunch. It's substantial enough to be a meal by itself, but try it topped with wedges of leftover samosas (or samusas, as they're called in Burma) and falafel, as they do at the restaurant. Because Burma shares borders with India, China, Laos, and Thailand, the country's cuisine contains elements of that of its neighbors–but it's the way these ingredients are combined that makes Burmese cooking truly unique.

TOTAL 45 MIN; SERVES 4

1 tsp. cumin seeds

1 tsp. black mustard seeds

⅓ cup vegetable oil

3 to 4 small chiles de árbol or other dried chiles

2 bay leaves

1 medium onion, finely chopped

¼ cup finely chopped garlic (about 12 garlic cloves)

1 Tbsp. kosher salt

1½ tsp. paprika

1 tsp. ground turmeric

½ cup water

¼ cup toasted chickpea flour

2 qt. vegetable broth

½ cup tamarind water

½ cup dried yellow lentils

1 medium russet potato, peeled and chopped

2 red Thai chiles or ½ jalapeño, chopped

½ tsp. garam masala

Chopped fresh mint, thinly sliced cabbage, fresh cilantro leaves, thinly sliced red Thai chiles, and lime wedges, for serving

1 Toast cumin and mustard seeds in a large, dry saucepan over medium, stirring often, until fragrant, about 30 seconds. Remove from heat, and grind into a coarse powder. Add oil to pan, and heat over medium-high. Add cumin mixture, chiles de árbol, and bay leaves, and cook, stirring constantly, until fragrant, about 25 seconds. Reduce heat to medium, and stir in onion. Cook, stirring occasionally, until onion softens, about 15 minutes. Stir in garlic, and cook, stirring often, until fragrant, about 2 minutes. Stir in salt, paprika, and turmeric.

2 Whisk together ½ cup water and chickpea flour in a small bowl until well combined. Add chickpea flour mixture, broth, tamarind water, lentils, and potato to pan. Stir to combine, and bring to a boil over medium-high. Reduce heat to medium-low, and simmer until lentils and potato are tender, about 20 minutes. Stir in Thai chiles and garam masala.

3 Garnish servings with chopped mint, sliced cabbage, cilantro leaves, sliced Thai chiles, and lime wedges. —*Desmond Tan*

NOTE: To make tamarind water, combine ¾ cup boiling water and 1 heaping tablespoon tamarind pulp. Let steep 1 minute. Mash with a fork, and let steep 3 minutes. Pour through a fine wire-mesh strainer into a bowl; discard solids.

SHRIMP AND CORN CHOWDER

We took a deep editorial dive into the islands, rain forests, and mountains of Ecuador in a 2001 article, and we asked chef and author Maricel Presilla of Zafra in New Jersey to give our readers the best examples of classic Ecuadoran food. Presilla shared her fantastic recipe for a coastal Ecuadoran shrimp soup made with grated plantain, which gives the soup a wonderfully light and creamy body. This classic soup is topped with a vibrant salsa made with corn, tomatoes, scallions, cilantro, and lime.

ACTIVE 1 HR; TOTAL 2 HR; SERVES 6

- 2 lb. peeled and deveined raw medium shrimp
- 2 scallions, minced
- 2 Tbsp. fresh lime juice
- 6 garlic cloves, minced, divided
- 1 tsp. kosher salt, plus more to taste
- 2 cups fresh or thawed frozen corn kernels
- 2 cups whole milk
- 2 Tbsp. Annatto Oil (recipe follows)
- 1 large red onion, finely chopped
- 1 large red bell pepper, finely chopped
- 1 tsp. ground cumin
- 3 plum tomatoes, peeled, seeded, and finely chopped
- 6 cups fish or chicken stock or canned low-sodium broth
- 1 green plantain, peeled and coarsely grated
- 2 Tbsp. fresh cilantro leaves
- ¼ tsp. cayenne pepper
  Tangy Corn Salsa (recipe follows)

1 Toss together shrimp, scallions, lime juice, two-thirds of the minced garlic, and salt in a large shallow glass or stainless-steel bowl. Cover with plastic wrap, and chill 1 hour or up to 3 hours.

2 Combine corn and milk in a food processor, and puree until smooth. Pour puree through a coarse strainer, pressing on solids to extract as much liquid as possible. Discard solids.

3 Heat annatto oil in a large saucepan or enameled cast-iron casserole dish over medium. Add remaining garlic, onion, bell pepper, and cumin, and cook, stirring often, until vegetables are slightly softened, about 5 minutes. Stir in tomatoes, and cook 2 minutes. Add corn milk, stock, plantain, cilantro, and cayenne, and bring to a boil. Simmer over medium-low until very flavorful, about 20 minutes.

4 Pour soup through a coarse strainer. Working in batches, puree solids in a blender. Return puree and strained broth to saucepan, and bring to a simmer over medium. Add shrimp and marinade, and cook until shrimp are just opaque, about 2 minutes. Season with salt to taste, and serve in warmed soup bowls with corn salsa. —*Maricel Presilla*

ANNATO OIL Combine 1 cup corn oil and ¼ cup annatto seeds in a small saucepan; bring to a simmer over low. Remove from heat, cover, and let cool completely. Strain oil into a jar; discard solids.

TANGY CORN SALSA Bring a small saucepan of salted water to a boil; add 1 cup fresh or thawed corn kernels, and cook just until tender, about 3 minutes for fresh or 1 minute for frozen. Drain and let cool; pat dry. Toss together corn; 3 plum tomatoes, peeled, seeded, and finely chopped; 2 scallions, minced; 2 Tbsp. coarsely chopped fresh cilantro; and 2½ Tbsp. fresh lime juice in a small bowl. Season with kosher salt and freshly ground black pepper, and let stand at least 1 hour before serving.

NOTE Annatto Oil can be refrigerated in a tightly sealed jar up to 2 months.

WINE Pair with a lime-scented dry Riesling.

MARICEL PRESILLA

t is not surprising that Maricel Presilla's favorite cookbook is a 14th-century Catalan cookbook called *Libre de Sent Soví*.

"It's a collection of medieval Spanish recipes that I turn to again and again," she says. "With help from that book and others like it, I've been able to trace the history of Latin American ingredients and techniques back to Spain."

The Cuban-born Presilla—who holds a doctorate in medieval Spanish history from New York University—is as much a culinary historian as she is a chef. A passion for research and love for the kitchen has pretty much defined her life. It was in the '80s, when she was pursuing her doctorate, that she started cooking professionally under the tutelage of Felipe Rojas-Lombardi, a Peruvian-born chef who owned The Ballroom in Manhattan. The Ballroom was the first tapas restaurant in the United States.

One day Presilla dropped by The Ballroom kitchen to visit a friend. "Felipe saw us and joked, 'If you're going to be here more than 15 minutes, you have to cook some-thing.' So I made flans, and they sold out. I remember looking at the guests, astounded, and thinking: These people are actually paying for my flan!"

Rojas-Lombardi invited Presilla to come in and cook on her days off. She helped him with some writing, and he taught her how to write recipes. "He was my cooking school," she says.

Since then, she has devoted her career to spreading the word about Latin Ameri-can ingredients and cuisines. She has authored five books on various aspects of the subject and is the co-owner of two Latin American restaurants—Zafra and Cucharam-ama, both in Hoboken, New Jersey. She was named Best Chef Mid-Atlantic by the James Beard Foundation in 2012. Her book, *Gran Cocina Latina: The Food of Latin America*, was named Cookbook of the Year the following year.

She is fond of a Spanish phrase, "cocina de autor," she says, "the idea that, in the kitchen, we are authors—recording, writing, adapting, and editing along the way. I

VEGETABLE HOT-AND-SOUR SOUP

F&W often covered (and tried to debunk) diet trends, with columns on everything from avoiding carbs in the 1970s to embracing healthy fats in the 2010s. In a regular column on low-fat cooking, chef and author Eileen Yin-Fei Lo shared her recipes for Chinese food and tips to avoid hidden fat in marinades, sauces, and soups. Her Vegetable Hot-and-Sour Soup offers extraordinary depth of flavor from ginger, soy sauce, and sesame oil, plus layers of texture from lily buds, mushrooms, and bamboo shoots–you won't miss the meat.

ACTIVE 25 MIN; TOTAL 50 MIN; SERVES 4

40 dried lily buds (about ½ oz.)

¼ cup small dried tree ear mushrooms or dried shiitake mushroom caps

5 cups unsalted chicken stock or canned low-sodium broth

½ cup drained canned bamboo shoots, rinsed and julienned

2 tsp. minced peeled fresh ginger

½ tsp. kosher salt

3 Tbsp. red wine vinegar

1 tsp. crushed red pepper

3 Tbsp. cornstarch

3 Tbsp. water

1 large egg

1 large egg white

4 oz. firm tofu, drained and cut into ⅓-inch cubes

2½ Tbsp. soy sauce

1 tsp. toasted sesame oil

2 Tbsp. thinly sliced scallions (from 1 medium scallion)

1 Place lily buds and mushrooms in a small bowl; add very hot water to cover by 1 inch. Let soak until softened, about 30 minutes. Drain and rinse thoroughly. Trim and discard tough ends from buds, and cut in half crosswise. Coarsely chop mushrooms.

2 Stir together lily buds, mushrooms, chicken stock, bamboo shoots, ginger, and salt in a large nonreactive saucepan over high. Cover and bring to a boil. Reduce heat to medium, and simmer 10 minutes. Stir in vinegar and red pepper; increase heat to medium-high; boil for 2 minutes.

3 Whisk together cornstarch and 3 tablespoons water in a small bowl. Whisk cornstarch mixture into chicken stock mixture in a slow, steady stream; cook 1 minute. Beat together egg and egg white in a medium bowl. Pour egg mixture into chicken stock mixture in a slow, steady stream, stirring gently. Stir in tofu, soy sauce, and sesame oil, and cook, stirring occasionally, until warmed, about 2 minutes. Sprinkle with scallions before serving. —*Eileen Yin-Fei Lo*

NOTE Dried lily buds, also called tiger lily buds or golden needles, are nutritious and slightly sweet. Find dried lily buds and dried tree ear mushrooms at Asian markets. In Chinese dishes, they are often used with the dried fungi known as tree ear, or wood ear, mushrooms. Although both add layers of chewy texture to this dish, they can be omitted.

WINE Pair with a berry-inflected rosé.

CHERRY GAZPACHO

This truly delicious and unusual gazpacho from food writer Anya Von Bremzen is inspired by Andalusian chef Dani García, who includes sweet cherries in the mix, then tops the summery soup with shaved goat cheese "snow." The additional garnish of pistachios, basil oil, and piquant anchovy is a fine complement to the sweetness of the cherries.

ACTIVE 30 MIN; TOTAL 5 HR 30 MIN; SERVES 6

2 lb. ripe tomatoes, cored and chopped

½ lb. sweet cherries, pitted

1 small Italian frying pepper or Cubanelle pepper, stemmed, seeded, and chopped

1½ cups day-old cubed crustless rustic white bread (2 oz.)

⅓ cup chopped red onion

¼ cup sherry vinegar

1 garlic clove, finely chopped

½ cup plus ⅓ cup extra-virgin olive oil, divided

Pinch of kosher salt

Pinch of black pepper

1 cup packed basil leaves

Slivered anchovy fillets, chopped pistachios, and grated frozen goat cheese, for garnish

1 Toss tomatoes, cherries, Italian pepper, bread, onion, vinegar, garlic, ½ cup oil, and a very generous pinch each of salt and pepper in a large bowl. Let gazpacho base stand at room temperature for 2 hours.

2 Working in batches, puree gazpacho base until very smooth, about 2 minutes. Transfer to another large bowl. Cover and refrigerate at least 3 hours or overnight.

3 Meanwhile, blanch basil in a small saucepan of simmering water until tender, about 1 minute. Drain well, and cool under running water. Squeeze out excess moisture, and transfer to a blender. With machine on, gradually add remaining ⅓ cup of oil until mixture is bright green and very smooth. Pour liquid through a fine wire-mesh strainer into a small bowl; season basil oil with salt.

4 Season gazpacho with salt, adding tablespoons of water if too thick. To serve, ladle soup into bowls, and garnish with slivered anchovy fillets, chopped pistachios, grated frozen goat cheese, and basil oil. —*Anya Von Bremzen*

MAKE AHEAD The gazpacho can be refrigerated up to 3 days. Add a bit of water if it's too thick.

Salads

ESCAROLE SALAD WITH RED QUINOA AND HAZELNUTS

Food Network chef and New York restaurateur Marco Canora likes quinoa, a high-protein seed, because it mimics the satisfying texture and starchiness of a grain. We love this fresh winter salad—the pleasing bitterness of the escarole balanced by the sweet-tart flavor of the apple and, mostly, the sheer crunchiness of it all. It will become a perennial favorite with any kind of pork.

ACTIVE 20 MIN; TOTAL 40 MIN; SERVES 4 TO 6

¼ cup red quinoa, rinsed and drained

¼ cup plus 2 Tbsp. extra-virgin olive oil

3 Tbsp. apple cider vinegar

1 Tbsp. plus 1 tsp. honey

Fine sea salt

Black pepper

1 head of escarole, chopped into bite-size pieces

1 Granny Smith apple, halved, cored, and thinly sliced on a mandoline

½ cup toasted hazelnuts, chopped

1 Bring a medium saucepan of salted water to a boil; whisk in quinoa, and cook until tender, about 10 minutes. Drain well, and spread out on a baking sheet to cool.

2 Whisk the oil, vinegar, and honey in a large bowl. Season with salt and pepper. Add the escarole, apple, hazelnuts, and quinoa; toss to coat. Season with salt and pepper, and serve. —*Marco Canora*

BAKED GOAT CHEESE SALAD

Alice Waters used to say that she would rather make salads than almost anything else, which explains how she is responsible for one of the most iconic dishes of the late 1980s and 1990s, her baked goat cheese salad. In its essence, it's a harmonious blend of lettuces combined with softly baked thyme-and-breadcrumb-coated goat cheese, served alongside crunchy garlic croutons. As with so much of Alice Waters' seasonal, ingredient-driven cooking, this simple dish is all about the quality of the raw materials. Waters once said, "Only the best is good enough." So use the very best you can find. Marinating the goat cheese rounds in herb-infused olive oil ensures the cheese stays moist and browns evenly when baked.

ACTIVE 20 MIN; TOTAL 20 MIN, PLUS 8 HR REFRIGERATION; SERVES 4

1 (8-oz.) goat cheese log
¾ cup extra-virgin olive oil, divided, plus more for greasing
3 thyme sprigs
½ cup plain dry breadcrumbs
½ tsp. dried thyme
¼ cup red wine vinegar
Kosher salt
Freshly ground black pepper
8 cups loosely packed lettuce leaves
Garlic Croutons (recipe follows)

1 Divide goat cheese into 4 or 8 equal portions, and shape into ½-inch-thick rounds. Place goat cheese rounds in a shallow glass dish; drizzle with ¼ cup oil, and turn to coat completely. Top with thyme sprigs. Cover and refrigerate 8 hours or overnight.

2 Preheat oven to 400°F. Stir together breadcrumbs and thyme in a small bowl. Remove cheese rounds from oil, and coat thoroughly with breadcrumb mixture. Transfer to a lightly greased baking sheet. Bake in preheated oven until golden brown and bubbly, 10 to 12 minutes.

3 Meanwhile, place vinegar in a small bowl, and season with salt and pepper; whisk in remaining ½ cup oil.

4 Toss lettuce leaves with vinaigrette to lightly coat. Mound dressed lettuce on each of 4 plates. Top each with warm goat cheese rounds. Serve immediately with croutons. —*Alice Waters*

GARLIC CROUTONS Preheat oven to 350°F. Brush both sides of 24 ¼-inch-thick day-old baguette slices with ¼ cup melted unsalted butter, then place in a single layer on a baking sheet. Bake in preheated oven until golden brown, about 15 minutes, turning halfway through baking. Rub croutons with cut sides of 2 medium garlic cloves while croutons are slightly warm. —*Alice Waters*

WINE Pair with a Loire Valley Sauvignon Blanc.

ALICE WATERS

Today, there are very few chefs anywhere in the world that command the respect Alice Waters does. When she opened Chez Panisse in Berkeley, California, in 1971, no one—certainly not the chef herself—had an inkling that what she created there would explode into a culinary movement. Waters was inspired by the fresh, simple foods she cooked and ate studying abroad in France as a French Cultural Studies major at UC Berkeley. The California spin that Waters and her team at Chez Panisse put on French cooking was new, and it was her insistence on fresh, seasonal ingredients—an idea that seems so basic today, yet at the time was quite novel—that truly set her apart.

For Waters, the kitchen was not where she thought she'd end up. "When I graduated from college it was just kind of expected you would get married and have children.... It never occurred to me that I would go down another path." But she did, and she did it with little experience in the kitchen. Waters readily admits that she and the women she opened Chez Panisse with (Victoria Wise, the first chef, and Lindsey here, the pastry chef) were not chefs by trade or by education. "We didn't operate the restaurant the way we were expected to. We were cooking the way that we cooked at home." The way they were cooking endured, became celebrated, then emulated.

Shortly after the James Beard Awards began, Waters was quickly recognized for her work. At the second annual Beards Awards in 1992, she picked up an award for both outstanding chef and outstanding restaurant.

Her legacy reaches all over the food world. Her work championing farmers and fresh seasonal food endures and has truly changed the way many of us cook and eat.

CAESAR SALAD
WITH TORN CROUTONS

Caesar salad may be a classic, but that doesn't mean you can't play it up a bit. There is so much good to be said about British chef and New York restaurateur April Bloomfield's version: Plenty of salty anchovies and Parmigiano-Reggiano punch up the dressing, and we love Little Gem lettuce in place of typical romaine here.

ACTIVE 25 MIN; TOTAL 1 HR; SERVES 6

½ lb. day-old rustic Italian bread, crusts discarded and bread torn into bite-size pieces

10 anchovy fillets, plus more for garnish

¼ cup red wine vinegar

3 Tbsp. Dijon mustard

2 garlic cloves

1 large egg

1 cup vegetable oil

⅓ cup freshly grated Parmigiano-Reggiano cheese, plus more for serving

Kosher salt

Freshly ground black pepper

18 oz. Little Gem lettuce, leaves separated and chilled

1 Preheat oven to 400°F. Spread bread pieces on a rimmed baking sheet, and bake until golden and crisp, about 12 minutes; let croutons cool.

2 Meanwhile, combine anchovy fillets, vinegar, mustard, and garlic in a food processor; puree until smooth. Add egg and pulse just until incorporated. With machine running, gradually drizzle in oil until emulsified. Scrape dressing into a bowl, and stir in grated cheese. Season with salt and pepper. Cover dressing with plastic wrap, and refrigerate until well chilled and thickened, at least 30 minutes.

3 Toss chilled lettuce leaves with half the dressing in a large bowl; gently massage to coat. (Save remaining dressing for another salad or to serve with grilled chicken.) Arrange dressed lettuce on a platter, and scatter croutons on top. Garnish with anchovy fillets, and serve right away, passing shredded Parmigiano cheese at the table. —April Bloomfield

WINE Pair with a vibrant, medium-bodied white, like a white Bordeaux blend.

PERSIMMON, POMEGRANATE, AND PURSLANE WITH PEPITAS

Suzanne Goin, the chef at the famed Lucques in Los Angeles–and a *F&W* Best New Chef in 1999–marked 20 years of business in 2018 with a dinner that celebrated her now-classic blend of French cuisine and California produce. Goin refers to this salad as "The 4 Ps" and thinks of it as a persimmon salad with an arugula garnish, rather than the other way around. We love that it celebrates a season and a place with such a gorgeous jumble of flavors and colors.

ACTIVE 10 MIN; TOTAL 20 MIN; SERVES 6

2 Tbsp. fresh lime juice

1 Tbsp. minced shallot

1 Tbsp. fresh orange juice

½ cup extra-virgin olive oil

4 large or 6 small Fuyu persimmons (about 1 lb.), cut into ¼-inch wedges

Kosher salt

Freshly ground black pepper

1 bunch young arugula (about 2 cups), rinsed and dried

1 cup purslane sprigs

6 Tbsp. pomegranate arils

6 Tbsp. salted roasted pepitas

1 Combine lime juice, shallot, and orange juice in a bowl. Let stand 10 minutes. Whisk in oil.

2 Place persimmons in a large bowl, and season with salt and pepper. Add dressing, and toss gently to coat. Season arugula and purslane with salt and pepper, and gently toss with dressed persimmons. Divide salad among six plates, and top with pomegranate arils and pepitas. —*Suzanne Goin*

WINE Pair with a medium-bodied, almondy Verdicchio.

CRISPY OKRA SALAD

Is any other vegetable as polarizing as okra? Much maligned, it definitely falls into the love-it-or-hate-it category, and even the food-loving *F&W* team has some naysayers. But this method for preparing okra, where it's sliced into thin strips and fried until crispy, sways even the biggest haters. Melissa Rubel Jacobson, former *F&W* Test Kitchen associate, says, "I hated okra, but I had never tried it like this before. It was a total eye-opener." The salad is the brainchild of Indian chef Suvir Saran, who first thought to cut the vegetable into strips and not rounds when he was just a kid. As an adult, he took it one step further and incorporated crispy okra into a spiced salad with crunchy onions and fresh tomatoes.

TOTAL 50 MIN; SERVES 4

1¼ tsp. garam masala

¼ tsp. amchoor powder (optional)

Vegetable oil, for frying

1 lb. young okra, halved lengthwise and cut into long, thin strips

Kosher salt

½ small red onion, very thinly sliced

1 medium tomato, cored, seeded, and cut into thin strips

¼ cup coarsely chopped fresh cilantro

2 Tbsp. fresh lemon juice

1 Stir together garam masala and, if desired, amchoor powder in a small bowl.

2 Heat 1 inch of oil in a large, deep skillet to 350°F. Working in batches, fry okra strips, stirring occasionally, until golden and crisp, about 4 minutes per batch. Using a slotted spoon, transfer the fried okra to a large paper-towel-lined plate to drain. Sprinkle each batch lightly with some of the spice mixture and salt.

3 Gently toss together fried okra, onion, tomato, cilantro, and lemon juice in a large bowl. Season salad with more spice mixture and salt, and serve immediately.
—*Suvir Saran*

NOTE Amchoor powder, which is made from dried green mangoes, adds a fruity, tangy note to this dish.

WINE Pair with an off-dry, minerally German Riesling.

TOMATOES WITH HERBS AND ALMOND VINAIGRETTE

When we come across a recipe that is both delicious and economical, we take notice. An eye-opener for us was the vinaigrette that chef Dan Kluger of New York City's Loring Place created for this salad, which highlights summer's juiciest and sweetest tomatoes. Kluger (who was named a Best New Chef in 2012 for his work at New York's ABC Kitchen) toasts chopped almonds in olive oil until crisp and golden, then, instead of discarding that fragrant oil, he whisks in grated garlic, vinegar, lime juice, and a bit of sugar for a phenomenal dressing. Topped with red onion, jalapeño, mint, and basil, this dish is a total summer showstopper.

TOTAL 45 MIN; SERVES 4

- 6 Tbsp. extra-virgin olive oil
- ½ cup almonds, coarsely chopped and sifted to remove crumbs
- 1 garlic clove, finely grated
- ¼ cup red wine vinegar
- 2 Tbsp. fresh lime juice
- 1 tsp. granulated sugar
  Kosher salt
  Freshly ground black pepper
- 2 lb. heirloom tomatoes, some sliced and some halved
- ⅓ cup very thinly sliced red onion, soaked in ice water 10 minutes
- ½ small jalapeño, minced
- ¼ cup torn fresh mint
- ¼ cup torn fresh Thai basil

1 Heat oil in a medium skillet over medium-low. Add almonds, and cook, stirring occasionally, until well browned, about 7 minutes. Pour through a fine wire-mesh strainer into a heatproof bowl; reserve almonds. Immediately whisk garlic into warm oil, and let cool slightly. Whisk in vinegar, lime juice, and sugar. Season dressing with salt and pepper.

2 Spread tomatoes on a large platter. Season with salt, and let stand 5 minutes.

3 Drain onions; pat dry. Scatter onions over tomatoes, then drizzle with dressing, and sprinkle with jalapeño, mint, basil, and almonds. —*Dan Kluger*

WINE Pair with a vibrant Provençal rosé.

WARM SUMMER VEGETABLE SALAD WITH BROWN BUTTER DRESSING

In this exquisitely simple recipe, Portland, Oregon, chef Gabriel Rucker brilliantly riffs on the classic combination of radish, butter, and salt by tossing wedges of crunchy radish in a warm dressing made with brown butter (instead of oil) and Spanish Moscatel vinegar (which is golden and slightly bittersweet). This was the first time we had seen a recipe using nutty browned butter in place of oil to dress a salad. Needless to say, we loved it.

TOTAL 45 MIN; SERVES 4

2 small leeks or 16 baby leeks, white and tender green parts only, halved and washed

½ lb. green beans

4 cups baby arugula (2 oz.)

2½ Tbsp. unsalted butter

¼ cup Moscatel, white balsamic, or late-harvest wine vinegar

¼ cup thinly sliced red onion

16 small radishes, quartered

Kosher salt

Freshly ground black pepper

¼ cup small or torn fresh mint leaves

1 Bring a medium saucepan of salted water to a boil. Add leeks, cover, and simmer on low until tender, about 10 minutes (3 minutes for baby leeks). Using a slotted spoon, transfer leeks to a paper-towel-lined plate to drain. Cut leeks lengthwise into long, thin strands.

2 Add beans to saucepan. Cook just until tender, 4 minutes. Drain and pat dry.

3 Put arugula in a large bowl. Heat butter in a large skillet over medium-high until richly browned, about 2 minutes. Add leeks, green beans, vinegar, onion, and radishes, and toss until warmed. Spoon vegetables and butter dressing over arugula, toss well, and season with salt and pepper. Arrange salad on 4 plates, garnish with mint leaves, and serve. —*Gabriel Rucker*

ANTIPASTO SALAD WITH GREEN OLIVE TAPENADE

Nancy Silverton, cofounder of Campanile and La Brea Bakery (for which she was named Best New Chef in 1990) and co-owner of Osteria Mozza and Pizzeria Mozza in Los Angeles, is famous for her baking. She's also a master of Italian flavors. Case in point: this smart and delicious play on a classic antipasto plate. Shredded iceberg lettuce serves as the crunchy base for a salad made with creamy mozzarella balls (bocconcini), Genoa salami, peperoncini, and green olives. It's one of those "Why didn't I think of that?" dishes that hits all the right notes. Serve with crusty bread and make it a meal.

TOTAL 25 MIN; SERVES 8

¼ cup peperoncini, stemmed, seeded, and finely chopped

½ cup extra-virgin olive oil, divided

3 Tbsp. jarred green olive tapenade

1½ cups bocconcini (about 9 oz.)

4 tsp. fresh lemon juice

4 tsp. red wine vinegar

4 tsp. minced garlic

1 tsp. dried oregano

Kosher salt

Freshly ground black pepper

1 small head iceberg lettuce, halved, cored, and finely shredded (about 4 cups)

6 oz. thinly sliced Genoa salami, cut into thin strips (about 1½ cups)

½ cup green olives, such as picholine

6 small, fresh basil leaves

1 Stir together peperoncini, ¼ cup oil, and tapenade in a medium bowl. Add bocconcini, and toss to combine.

2 Whisk together lemon juice, vinegar, garlic, and oregano in a small bowl. Whisk in remaining ¼ cup oil; season with salt and pepper.

3 Combine lettuce, salami, bocconcini mixture, and half the vinaigrette in a bowl; toss well to combine. Transfer salad to a large platter. Top with olives and basil leaves. Drizzle with remaining vinaigrette. —*Nancy Silverton*

MAKE AHEAD The recipe can be prepared through Step 2 and refrigerated overnight.

WINE Pair with a medium-bodied, aromatic Albariño.

NANCY SILVERTON

Nancy Silverton trained professionally as a baker, not a cook. And although she made her name with breads and desserts at Los Angeles's Campanile and the legendary La Brea Bakery—at the forefront of the artisanal bread movement in this country—her culinary genius may very well lie in her incredible palate. Many who have eaten Silverton's food, not just her baked goods, describe having rapturous gustatory experiences.

"If someone asked me to fillet a whole fish, I wouldn't have a clue," she says. "But if I taste a dish, I'll know exactly what it needs." Like a chemist, she might add a drop of lemon juice or a scattering of sea salt to "bring the flavor to another level."

Born and raised in Southern California, Silverton enrolled in Sonoma State University as a political science major, but in her freshman year experienced an epiphany cooking vegetarian food in the dorms: She wanted to be a chef. She dropped out of college her senior year and went to London to train at Le Cordon Bleu. Upon returning to Southern California, she perfected her pastry skills in some of L.A.'s most storied kitchens—including Spago, where she worked under Wolfgang Puck.

Experimenting with flours, yeast starters, bake times, and doughs led to the founding of La Brea in 1989, where her iconic sourdough starter recipe was created. Although Silverton and La Brea have since parted ways, Silverton has achieved a series of successes. She's racked up several James Beard Awards and is the co-owner of a handful of restaurants.

Her most lasting legacy, though, might be her role in giving Americans a taste for really good bread.

FARRO AND GREEN OLIVE SALAD
WITH WALNUTS AND RAISINS

When food bloggers hit the scene, a whole new slew of talent became part of the pages of *F&W*. Among the first of those was Heidi Swanson, who started writing her wonderful vegetarian food blog, 101 Cookbooks, in 2003. Swanson was also at the forefront of the whole-grain craze, and her incredible farro and green olive salad was featured in our "Salad of the Month" column. The secret is in the balance: Each bite holds a bit of chewy farro, toasty walnut, fresh scallion, and briny green olive. Swanson's dressing is a little sweet and a little spicy, and, put together, it's an explosion of flavor and texture that's unbeatable.

TOTAL 40 MIN; SERVES 6 TO 8

1¼ cups farro (about ½ lb.)
4 cups water
½ tsp. fine sea salt, plus more to taste
1 cup walnuts (about 3½ oz.)
2½ cups pitted green olives, preferably Castelvetrano, chopped
4 scallions, white and light green parts only, finely chopped
⅓ cup snipped fresh chives
¼ cup extra-virgin olive oil
3 Tbsp. fresh lemon juice
2 Tbsp. golden raisins
1 Tbsp. honey
½ tsp. crushed red pepper
  Shaved Pecorino cheese, for serving

1 Preheat oven to 375°F. Place farro in a medium saucepan; add 4 cups water and salt, and bring to a boil. Reduce heat to maintain a simmer, and cook, partially covered, until farro is tender, about 20 minutes. Drain farro in a fine wire-mesh strainer, and spread on a baking sheet to let cool.

2 Meanwhile, place walnuts in a pie plate, and toast in preheated oven until lightly golden and fragrant, 5 to 7 minutes. Let cool, then coarsely chop.

3 Combine farro, walnuts, olives, scallions, chives, oil, lemon juice, raisins, honey, and red pepper in a large bowl, and season with salt. Toss well. Transfer salad to a platter, and garnish with shaved cheese. —*Heidi Swanson*

MAKE AHEAD The salad can be refrigerated overnight. Bring salad to room temperature before serving.

WINE Pair with a ripe, citrusy California Sauvignon Blanc.

WINTER CHICORY SALAD WITH KUMQUATS AND DATE DRESSING

At Jardinière in San Francisco, chef-owner Traci Des Jardins is constantly looking for dishes with a balance of sweet, acid, and salt. This recipe hits all those notes for a crunchy, salty, sweet, bitter winter salad. A mix of young chicories, like endive, frisée, and radicchio, makes for a blast of color welcome during colder months. If kumquats are unavailable, use paper-thin slices of unpeeled clementines.

TOTAL 20 MIN; SERVES 6

½ cup extra-virgin olive oil

3 Tbsp. sherry vinegar

3 Tbsp. fresh orange juice

1 Tbsp. finely chopped shallot

2 cups kumquats, sliced into ⅛-inch rounds, seeds removed, divided

½ cup dried pitted dates, thinly sliced, divided

1 tsp. kosher salt, divided

½ tsp. black pepper, divided

4 Belgian endive leaves, sliced (about 1 cup)

2 cups bright yellow frisée leaves (from 1 large head, use yellow leaves only)

2 cups packed fresh arugula

1 cup packed fresh mizuna

1 cup sliced Treviso or Chioggia radicchio

½ cup loosely packed fresh flat-leaf parsley leaves

1 Tbsp. fresh mint leaves, cut into thin strips

½ cup toasted salted pistachios

4 oz. aged Pecorino Romano cheese, shaved with a Y-shape vegetable peeler (about 2 cups)

1 Whisk together olive oil, sherry vinegar, orange juice, shallot, 1 tablespoon kumquats, and 1 tablespoon dates in a medium bowl until blended. Season with ½ teaspoon salt and ¼ teaspoon pepper.

2 Place remaining kumquats and dates in a large bowl. Reserve and set aside 6 tablespoons vinaigrette. Drizzle remaining vinaigrette over kumquat mixture, and, using your hands, pull dates apart into individual slices. Add endive, frisée, arugula, mizuna, radicchio, parsley, and mint; gently toss to coat. Season with remaining ½ teaspoon salt and remaining ¼ teaspoon pepper.

3 To serve, divide salad evenly among 6 plates; drizzle 1 tablespoon of the reserved vinaigrette over top and around each salad. Garnish with pistachios and shaved Pecorino Romano. —*Traci Des Jardins*

RICE NOODLE SALAD
BOWLS WITH GRILLED
LEMONGRASS CHICKEN

We love this fresh and light dish from cookbook author and teacher Andrea Nguyen because it is an absolute riot of textures, temperatures, and flavors that can be customized in nearly limitless ways. Like rice paper rolls and banh mi, rice-noodle salad bowls–often categorized at restaurants as rice vermicelli bowls or bun ("boon," the name of the noodles in Vietnamese)–can feature many wonderful things, like grilled lemongrass chicken skewers. Simply layer the ingredients in a bowl and let diners dress and mix up their own at the table. The vegetables provide refreshing crunch and herbal pungency, the noodles carry flavor, and the main feature and toppings are up to you. Grilled chicken skewers are the highlight here. Nuoc Cham unites things with its Viet imprint.

TOTAL 1 HR; SERVES 4

MARINADE

- ¼ cup coarsely chopped lemongrass (from 1 medium stalk)
- 3 Tbsp. coarsely chopped shallot
- 1½ Tbsp. granulated sugar or 2 Tbsp. light brown sugar
- 1½ Tbsp. canola oil, grapeseed oil, or other neutral oil
- 1½ Tbsp. fish sauce
- 1 Tbsp. chopped garlic
- 1 tsp. soy sauce
- ⅜ tsp. cayenne pepper or black pepper

SALAD BOWLS

- 1¼ lb. boneless, skinless chicken thighs, cut into 3- x 1-inch strips
- 10 (5-inch) skewers
- 1 (6- to 8-oz.) pkg. dried rice stick noodles or 1 (10- to 12-oz.) pkg. dried rice capellini pasta or thin spaghetti
- 4 cups loosely packed mixed baby lettuces or soft-leaf lettuce leaves, thinly sliced
- 1⅓ cups fresh bean sprouts (optional)
- 1 (2-oz.) Persian cucumber, shaved into thin strips (optional)
- ½ cup torn fresh cilantro, divided
- ½ cup torn fresh mint, basil, and/or dill, divided
  Canola oil, grapeseed oil, or other neutral oil, for brushing
- ⅔ cup unsalted roasted peanuts or cashews, coarsely chopped
- ¼ cup crispy fried shallots or onions (optional)
- 1 cup Nuoc Cham (recipe follows)

1 MAKE THE MARINADE Combine lemongrass, shallot, sugar, oil, fish sauce, garlic, soy sauce, and cayenne in a food processor. Pulse until mixture resembles a slightly coarse puree, about 10 times. Transfer marinade to a large bowl.

2 MAKE THE SALAD BOWLS Add chicken to marinade; massage until coated. Thread chicken evenly onto skewers. Transfer skewers to a large plate; discard remaining marinade. Cover skewers; let stand at room temperature 30 minutes to 1 hour.

3 Meanwhile, boil noodles in a pot of water until chewy-tender. Drain and rinse under cold water; drain again. Divide lettuce and, if desired, bean sprouts and cucumber among 4 large serving bowls. Sprinkle bowls evenly with 6 tablespoons cilantro and 6 tablespoons mint, basil, and/or dill. Top evenly with noodles.

4 Heat a grill pan over medium-high. Lightly brush skewered chicken with oil. Cook chicken, turning occasionally, until slightly charred and cooked through, 8 to 12 minutes.

5 Divide chicken among noodle bowls (either on or off skewers). Top bowls evenly with peanuts; fried shallots, if desired; remaining 2 tablespoons cilantro; and remaining 2 tablespoons mint, basil, and/or dill. Place Nuoc Cham in a small bowl; let diners dress and toss their own bowls. —*Andrea Nguyen*

NUOC CHAM Stir together ½ cup water, 3 Tbsp. fresh lime juice, and 2 Tbsp. granulated sugar in a small bowl until sugar dissolves. Add additional lime juice and sugar to taste; dilute with water if flavors are too strong. If there's an unpleasant tart-bitter edge, add 2 tsp. rice vinegar. Stir in 3 Tbsp. fish sauce; add additional fish sauce to taste. If you like, stir in 2 Tbsp. grated or matchstick-cut carrot, 1½ tsp. minced garlic, and/or 1 thinly sliced unseeded serrano chile (or 2 to 3 tsp. sambal oelek). Serve sauce in a bowl on the table so diners may help themselves or divide among small individual bowls in advance. —*Andrea Nguyen*

MAKE AHEAD The sauce can stand at room temperature up to 8 hours before serving. Uncooked chicken skewers can be covered and refrigerated overnight; let come to room temperature before grilling. Noodles can be cooked, covered, and stored in the refrigerator up to 3 days; sprinkle with water, and microwave on HIGH for about 1 minute to soften and refresh.

NOTE If using wooden skewers and cooking over a live fire, soak the skewers in hot water for 20 minutes before using.

Potatoes & Vegetables

POTATO AND EGG PIE WITH
BACON AND CRÈME FRAÎCHE

Paula Wolfert is one of the earliest and steadiest contributors to *F&W*, bringing in stories and recipes from all over Europe and the Mediterranean. In one of her first features for the magazine, Wolfert penned an article about three great Alsatian chefs cooking their mothers' food. Included was André Soltner, then the chef-owner at the legendary Lutèce in Manhattan. Soltner opted to re-create his mother's potato pie, which Wolfert said was "a simple thing, yet elegant." It consisted of a flaky pâte brisée filled with thinly sliced potatoes, bacon, hard-cooked eggs, herbs, and crème fraîche. Wolfert noted how strongly Soltner felt while preparing the dish, with "pleasure and nostalgia ... plainly visible on his face." This is home cooking at its best from one of America's most revered French chefs. Paired with a green salad, this pie makes a very satisfying weekend lunch. In a pinch, use a store-bought pie crust.

ACTIVE 25 MIN; TOTAL 9 HR 45 MIN; SERVES 6

1¾ cups all-purpose flour (about 7½ oz.), plus more for dusting

9 Tbsp. cold unsalted butter, cubed

1 tsp. kosher salt, divided

2 large egg yolks, divided

Ice water

1¼ lb. Yukon Gold potatoes, peeled and thinly sliced (about 4 cups)

¼ cup finely chopped fresh flat-leaf parsley

¼ tsp. black pepper

5 oz. thick-cut mild-smoked bacon slices, cut into ¼-inch pieces

½ cup crème fraîche or sour cream

3 large or 4 small hard-cooked eggs, peeled and thinly sliced

1 tsp. water

1 Stir together flour, butter, and ¾ teaspoon salt in a large bowl. Using your fingertips, rub butter into flour mixture until mixture resembles coarse meal. Make a well in center. Stir together 1 egg yolk with enough ice water to equal ¼ cup; pour into well, and stir into flour mixture until just moistened. Turn dough out onto a lightly floured surface. Knead dough just until it comes together. Divide dough into 2 disks. Wrap each disk in plastic wrap, and chill at least 8 hours or overnight.

2 Preheat oven to 400°F with oven rack in middle of oven. Unwrap 1 dough disk, and roll into a 13-inch round on a lightly floured surface; fit into a 9-inch pie pan. Chill 10 minutes.

3 Meanwhile, soak potato slices in ice water to cover (to remove surface starch) about 5 minutes; drain and pat slices dry. Toss potatoes with parsley, pepper, and remaining ¼ teaspoon salt. Cook bacon in a large skillet over medium-high, stirring occasionally, until wilted and just browned on edges, about 2 minutes. Remove and drain on a plate lined with paper towels.

4 Arrange half the potato slices in refrigerated pie shell, overlapping slices. Sprinkle evenly with bacon; top with remaining potato slices, overlapping slices. Spread crème fraîche over potatoes, and arrange egg slices on top. Unwrap remaining dough disk, and roll into a 10-inch round on a lightly floured surface. Place round on top of pie. Trim edges and fold dough under. Crimp edge as desired. Using the tip of a knife, prick top of pie twice.

5 Stir together 1 teaspoon water and remaining egg yolk; brush over top of pie. Bake in preheated oven 20 minutes; reduce oven temperature to 350°F, and bake 50 minutes. Reduce oven temperature to 300°F, and bake until top is golden brown, about 10 minutes.

6 Let pie rest 10 minutes before serving. —*André Soltner*

SWEET POTATO CASSEROLE

This dessertlike sweet potato casserole from the late legendary chef and author Edna Lewis is a staple of Thanksgiving tables in the deep South, where it plays a crucial role in the balance of dishes on the table. While it's definitely lovely at the holidays, we love this just about any time.

ACTIVE 25 MIN; TOTAL 3 HR 5 MIN; SERVES 12

SWEET POTATOES

- 5 lb. sweet potatoes (about 10)
- 8 Tbsp. unsalted butter (4 oz.), cut into pieces, plus more for greasing
- ⅔ cup granulated sugar
- ½ cup packed light brown sugar
- ½ cup honey
- 2 tsp. pure vanilla extract
- 1¾ tsp. kosher salt
- ¾ tsp. freshly grated nutmeg
- 3 large eggs, lightly beaten
- 2½ cups hot milk

TOPPING

- 1 cup all-purpose flour (4¼ oz.)
- 1 cup packed light brown sugar
- ½ tsp. ground cinnamon
- ½ tsp. freshly grated nutmeg
- ¼ tsp. kosher salt
- 8 Tbsp. unsalted butter (4 oz.), chilled and cut into ½-inch dice
- 1 cup (4 oz.) coarsely chopped pecans

1 MAKE THE SWEET POTATOES Preheat oven to 350°F. Spread sweet potatoes on a rimmed baking sheet, and bake until tender, about 1½ hours. Let cool slightly, about 10 minutes, then peel.

2 Transfer the sweet potatoes to a large bowl; beat with an electric mixer on low speed. Beat in butter. Add granulated sugar, brown sugar, honey, vanilla, salt, and nutmeg and beat until blended. Add eggs and beat on medium speed for 2 minutes. Reduce speed to low and gradually add hot milk.

3 Preheat oven to 375°F. Butter a 9- x 13-inch baking dish, and pour in sweet potatoes; spread in an even layer.

4 MAKE THE TOPPING Combine flour, brown sugar, cinnamon, nutmeg, and salt in a bowl. Add butter and cut in until mixture resembles coarse meal. Stir in pecans.

5 Sprinkle topping evenly over potatoes, and bake until topping is golden brown and crisp, 1 to 1¼ hours. If topping browns too quickly around the edge before center is crisped, cut a large hole from the center of a sheet of foil and rest the foil on the edge of the dish while it finishes baking. Serve hot. —*Edna Lewis*

MAKE AHEAD The pureed sweet potato mixture and the topping can be refrigerated separately up to 1 day. Bring to room temperature before proceeding.

EDNA LEWIS (1916–2006)

She won the James Beard Living Legend Award. She's inspired a novel and a one-woman show. Her face even made its way onto a postage stamp. Known as the Grande Dame of Southern Cooking, Edna Lewis is responsible for shining a light on Southern cooking as the basis for American cuisine.

She was born and raised in Freetown, Virginia, a town established by emancipated slaves, including her own grandparents. In lyrical passages of her 1976 cookbook/memoir, *The Taste of Country Cooking*, she chronicles the changing seasons and the earth's bountiful harvest.

When she was just 16 years old, Lewis left her home and moved to Washington, D.C. Not long after, she relocated to New York City, where she eventually met Johnny Nicholson, with whom she would go on to open Café Nicholson in 1949.

At Cafe Nicholson, Lewis' culinary roots weren't lost on famous writers from the South who gravitated there. Truman Capote would beg her to make him biscuits. Her chocolate soufflé became famous. Lewis left Café Nicholson in the early 1950s. In 1972, she published her first cookbook, *The Edna Lewis Cookbook*.

Lewis worked in restaurants until late in life; she took a job at Brooklyn's Gage and Tollner when she was 72 years old. Eventually, she settled in Atlanta and met chef Scott Peacock, who became her companion and coauthor of her last cookbook, *The Gift of Southern Cooking: Recipes and Revelations from Two Great American Cooks* (2003).

Boston University gastronomy professor Megan Elias has written that "Edna Lewis wrote against that version of history in which African American cuisine makes the best of master's rations. She instead portrayed a culinary tradition that is distinctly chosen—hunted, foraged, and grown."

KIMCHI CREAMED COLLARD GREENS

"I don't think a cuisine should ever stop growing," says Hugh Acheson. And indeed, ever since he was named a Best New Chef in 2002, the chef has contributed dozens of super-tasty and smart updates on Southern classics to *F&W*. Among our favorites is this savory side dish of collards simmered with onion, bacon, chicken stock, vinegar, and sorghum, laced with a spicy kimchi cream sauce that gives the dish a funky kick.

ACTIVE 40 MIN; TOTAL 2 HR 15 MIN; SERVES 8

- 3 Tbsp. extra-virgin olive oil
- 1 large onion, cut into ¼-inch pieces
- ½ lb. bacon, cut into ¼-inch pieces
- 2 lb. stemmed collard greens, leaves cut into 2-inch pieces
- ¼ cup sherry vinegar
- 2 cups chicken stock
- 2 cups water
- 1 Tbsp. sorghum syrup or pure maple syrup
- ½ tsp. crushed red pepper
  Kosher salt
- 1 cup heavy cream
- 1 cup kimchi, finely chopped

1 Heat oil in a large pot or Dutch oven over medium. Add onion, and cook, stirring often, until golden brown, about 7 minutes. Add bacon, and cook, stirring often, until fat has rendered, about 10 minutes. Add collards, and cook over medium-high, stirring often, until collards begin to wilt, about 4 minutes. Add vinegar, and boil 1 minute. Add stock, 2 cups water, sorghum syrup, red pepper, and a generous pinch of salt. Cover and cook, stirring occasionally, until collards are very tender, about 1 hour and 30 minutes.

2 Meanwhile, bring cream to a simmer in a small saucepan over medium. Cook until reduced by one-third, about 10 minutes. Stir in kimchi, and remove from heat.

3 When collards are done, stir in kimchi cream, and season with salt to taste.
— *Hugh Acheson*

WINE Pair with an earthy cru Beaujolais, such as Morgon.

GRILLED GREENS WITH POPPED MUSTARD SEEDS AND GINGER

It's worth firing up the grill just to make this vegetable side from chef Biju Thomas of Biju's Little Curry Shop in Denver. Mustard greens blister and char over the hot grates until intensely smoky and crisp. He tops the greens with aromatics fried in coconut oil, followed by a squeeze of grilled lemon.

TOTAL 25 MIN; SERVES 4

- 2 bunches frilly mustard greens or kale
- 2 Tbsp. olive oil
- ½ tsp. kosher salt, plus more to taste
- 2 lemons, each cut into 4 wedges
- 5 Tbsp. coconut oil
- 1 Tbsp. black mustard seeds
- 10 curry leaves
- ¼ cup sliced shallots (from 2 medium shallots)
- 2 Tbsp. minced peeled fresh ginger
- 2 Tbsp. sliced garlic
- 2 serrano or Fresno chiles, cut into rings
- ¼ tsp. garam masala

1 Preheat grill to high (450°F to 500°F). Brush mustard greens with olive oil, and sprinkle with ½ teaspoon salt. Working in batches, grill greens in a single layer, uncovered, until blistered and charred, about 30 seconds. Flip, and grill until lightly charred and wilted, about 30 seconds. Transfer to a large baking sheet. Place lemon wedges, flesh side down, on grates, and grill, uncovered, until heated through and caramelized, about 3 minutes.

2 Remove any tough stems from greens. Arrange leaves on a large serving platter.

3 Melt coconut oil in a large skillet over medium-high. Add mustard seeds and curry leaves; cook, shaking skillet, until mustard seeds splatter and pop, about 30 seconds. Increase heat to high, and add shallots, ginger, garlic, and chiles. Cook, shaking skillet, until shallots are crisp and garlic is golden, 3 to 5 minutes. Spoon mixture over greens. Squeeze charred lemon wedges over greens. Sprinkle with garam masala, and add salt to taste. —*Biju Thomas*

MASHED POTATOES, KIND OF ROBUCHON-STYLE

In the November 2016 issue of *F&W*, the late Anthony Bourdain–chef, author, and travel documentarian–shared a secret: He loved Thanksgiving, and the more traditional the better. This is his version of Michelin-starred chef Joël Robuchon's famous supersilky, superrich, superlight, and buttery mashed potatoes. "This is not how the great chef Joël Robuchon makes his mashed potatoes," Bourdain wrote. "I have heard how from cooks who have worked for him, but they swore me to secrecy. What I do know for sure is there's a lot of butter in them–and that the way Robuchon actually makes them is too hard and too complicated for you (or me) to do sensibly at home. But this will approximate–roughly– the kind of buttery, ethereal suspension that dreams (and Joël Robuchon's mashed potatoes) are made of."

ACTIVE 30 MIN; TOTAL 1 HR; SERVES 8

4 lb. medium Yukon Gold potatoes, peeled and halved

Kosher salt

6 sticks cold unsalted butter (1½ lb.), cut into ½-inch cubes

½ cup heavy cream

1 Place potatoes in a large saucepan, and add water to cover; bring to a boil. Add 2 tablespoons of salt, and simmer until tender, 15 to 20 minutes. Drain well, and let stand in a colander for 3 minutes.

2 Pass the potatoes through a ricer into the large saucepan. Cook over medium, stirring until the potatoes are hot and steam starts to rise, about 2 minutes. Add one-fourth of the butter cubes at a time, stirring constantly until incorporated. Stir in the heavy cream and season generously with salt. Serve right away.
—*Anthony Bourdain*

ACORN SQUASH WITH COCONUT CUSTARD

Every year at Thanksgiving, the mother of *Top Chef* winner Kristen Kish would serve roasted acorn squash. When Kish took over cooking the holiday meal, she upgraded the classic side with a decadent coconut custard that offsets the earthy sweetness of the dish. It's not just great at Thanksgiving–it's wonderful as a special autumnal side dish at any dinner party. The custard will set as it cools and slices beautifully at room temperature.

ACTIVE 10 MIN; TOTAL 2 HR 15 MIN; SERVES 8

- 2 acorn squash, halved lengthwise, seeds removed
- 1 Tbsp. olive oil
- 1 tsp. kosher salt
- 6 fresh sage leaves, torn into small pieces
- 1 cup well-shaken and stirred canned coconut milk
- ½ cup heavy cream
- 4 large egg yolks
- ¼ cup granulated sugar
- 1 tsp. black pepper
- ½ tsp. orange zest
- ¼ tsp. fleur de sel
- 3 Tbsp. brown butter
- ¼ cup coarsely chopped walnuts, toasted

1 Preheat oven to 425°F. Cut a small slice off skin side of each squash half so they will sit flat while baking. Transfer to a large rimmed baking sheet.

2 Drizzle squash with oil, and season with salt; sprinkle evenly with sage. Roast until squash is tender and begins to brown, about 40 minutes. Let squash cool completely, about 30 minutes. Reduce oven temperature to 300°F.

3 Whisk together coconut milk, cream, egg yolks, sugar, pepper, orange zest, and fleur de sel in a large bowl until well combined. Pour coconut mixture evenly into well of each squash. Bake at 300°F until custard begins to set and jiggles slightly like gelatin, about 55 minutes. Let cool to room temperature, at least 1 hour and up to 3 hours. (As squash cools, custard will set up further.) Cut squash halves in half; transfer to a platter. Drizzle brown butter over top, and sprinkle with toasted walnuts. —*Kristen Kish*

CHICKPEAS AND KALE IN SPICY POMODORO SAUCE

This recipe from Missy Robbins of Brooklyn's award-winning Lilia restaurant turns classic pasta al pomodoro on its head. In her spicy, healthy, and irresistible version, Robbins (who was named a Best New Chef in 2010 for her cooking at A Voce) swaps out pasta in favor of nourishing chickpeas and tangles of kale. She says, "I created this dish when I was watching my weight, and I needed the satisfaction and flavor of a good red-sauce pasta—without using pasta. It's an amazing one-pan dish that's packed with richness but doesn't take a long time to make." For additional flavor, she tops the bowl with fresh herbs and salty Pecorino Romano.

TOTAL 45 MIN; SERVES 4

½ cup extra-virgin olive oil

5 garlic cloves, thinly sliced

1 (28-oz.) can whole peeled Italian tomatoes, crushed by hand

1 tsp. crushed red pepper

1½ tsp. fennel seeds

Kosher salt

1 (8-oz.) bunch lacinato kale, stemmed and chopped

2 (15-oz.) cans chickpeas, rinsed and drained

Torn fresh basil and marjoram, for garnish

Finely grated Pecorino Romano cheese, for serving

1 Heat oil in a large saucepan over low. Add garlic, and cook, stirring occasionally, until very fragrant but not browned, about 5 minutes. Add tomatoes, red pepper, fennel seeds, and a generous pinch of salt. Cook over medium-low, stirring occasionally, until tomatoes break down and sauce is thickened, about 25 minutes.

2 Stir kale into sauce, and cook over medium-low, stirring occasionally, until kale is wilted, about 3 minutes. Stir in chickpeas, and cook until heated through, about 3 minutes. Season with salt. Spoon into bowls, and garnish with basil and marjoram. Top with cheese, and serve hot. —*Missy Robbins*

WINE Pair with a savory, tea-leafy Chianti Classico.

BUTTERNUT SQUASH AND KALE
STRATA WITH MULTIGRAIN BREAD

The very best bread pudding meets stuffing in this decadent dish, which manages to be slightly healthy with the inclusion of multigrain bread, kale, and squash. It's a terrific make-ahead breakfast or brunch offering from baker and pastry chef Zoe Nathan of Huckleberry Cafe in Santa Monica.

ACTIVE 1 HR; TOTAL 3 HR; SERVES 8 TO 10

2½ Tbsp. unsalted butter, plus more
    for greasing

2 tsp. kosher salt, plus more to taste

½ tsp. freshly ground black pepper,
    plus more to taste

2 lb. butternut squash, peeled,
    seeded, and cut into ½-inch dice

¼ cup plus 1 Tbsp. extra-virgin olive oil

2 medium onions, thinly sliced, plus
    ½ small onion, finely chopped

¾ lb. kale, ribs discarded and
    leaves chopped

2 garlic cloves, minced
    Crushed red pepper

2 tsp. finely chopped thyme, divided

¼ cup all-purpose flour

2½ cups milk

1 cup heavy cream

½ cup crème fraîche

1 tsp. granulated sugar

8 large eggs

1 (¾-lb.) multigrain baguette, cut
    into 1-inch pieces

⅓ cup freshly grated
    Parmigiano-Reggiano cheese

1 Preheat oven to 425°F. Butter a 9- x 13-inch baking dish. Set aside. Toss squash with 2 tablespoons oil on a rimmed baking sheet, and season with salt and pepper. Bake, tossing once, until squash is just tender, for about 25 minutes. Reduce oven temperature to 325°F.

2 Meanwhile, heat 2 tablespoons oil in a large skillet. Add sliced onions, season with salt, and cook over medium-low, stirring occasionally, until golden, about 25 minutes. Scrape onions into a bowl.

3 Heat remaining 1 tablespoon oil, until shimmering, in the same skillet. Add kale, garlic, red pepper, and 1 teaspoon thyme, and season with salt. Cook over medium-high, tossing, until kale is wilted and just tender, about 5 minutes. Scrape kale into bowl with cooked onions.

4 Melt 2½ tablespoons butter in a medium saucepan. Add chopped onion and remaining 1 teaspoon thyme, and cook over medium-low, stirring, until softened, 5 minutes. Add flour, and cook over medium, whisking constantly, until a light golden paste forms, 3 minutes. Whisk in 1 cup milk, and cook, whisking, until very thick and no floury taste remains, 8 to 10 minutes. Remove from heat and whisk in cream, crème fraîche, sugar, 2 teaspoons salt, ½ teaspoon pepper, and remaining 1½ cups milk. Let béchamel cool.

5 Beat eggs into cooled béchamel in saucepan. Pour into a bowl, add bread and vegetables, and mix well. Pour strata mixture into prepared baking dish, and let stand for 30 minutes, pressing down bread occasionally.

6 Bake strata until almost set, 55 minutes to 1 hour at 325°F. Increase oven temperature to 475°F. Sprinkle Parmigiano on strata, and bake until top is lightly browned, about 10 minutes more. Let stand for 15 minutes before serving. —Zoe Nathan

MAKE AHEAD The strata can be prepared through Step 5 and refrigerated overnight.

ROASTED CURRY TOMATO PIE

As rustic as its appearance, this tomato pie from Samantha Fore, chef-owner of Tuk Tuk in Lexington, Kentucky, is a bonafide showstopper. Turmeric gives the rustic crust a glorious golden glow, but the real star (other than ripe summer tomatoes) is the sweet and tangy tamarind onions, which beautifully complement the spiced, cheesy filling.

TOTAL 1 HR 55 MIN; SERVES 8

PASTRY CRUST

- 1½ cups all-purpose flour (about 6⅜ oz.), plus more for work surface
- 1 tsp. kosher salt (½ tsp. if using Morton's kosher salt)
- ½ tsp. ground turmeric
- ½ tsp. black pepper
- ½ cup cold unsalted butter (4 oz.), cubed
- 4 to 5 Tbsp. ice water

TAMARIND ONIONS

- 2 Tbsp. canola oil
- ½ large red onion, thinly sliced into half-moons
- ½ tsp. kosher salt
- ½ tsp. black pepper
- ½ tsp. crushed red pepper
- 1 Tbsp. tamarind concentrate

FILLING

- 2 lb. ripe, red, medium-size and cherry tomatoes
- ½ Tbsp. Madras curry powder
- 1 tsp. kosher salt, divided
- 8 oz. low-moisture mozzarella cheese, shredded (about 2 cups)
- 2 oz. sharp white cheddar cheese, shredded (about ½ cup)
- ½ medium red onion, finely chopped
- ½ cup mayonnaise
- 1 serrano chile, stemmed, seeded, and finely chopped
- ½ tsp. crushed red pepper
- 1 Tbsp. olive oil
- 1 large egg, lightly beaten

1 MAKE THE PASTRY CRUST Combine flour, salt, turmeric, and black pepper in a food processor; pulse until combined. Add butter, and pulse until mixture is crumbly and butter is cut into small bits, about 10 times. Slowly add 4 tablespoons ice water while pulsing, adding up to 1 more tablespoon ice water, 1 teaspoon at a time, until dough comes together and forms a ball. Wrap in plastic wrap, and refrigerate until chilled, about 30 minutes.

2 MAKE THE TAMARIND ONIONS Heat canola oil in a large skillet over medium-high until shimmering. Stir in onion, salt, black pepper, and red pepper. Cook, stirring often, until onion is translucent, about 10 minutes. Stir in tamarind concentrate until combined. Remove from heat, and set aside.

3 MAKE THE FILLING Preheat oven to 400°F. Line a large rimmed baking sheet with 2 layers of paper towels. Cut medium-size tomatoes into ½-inch-thick slices; cut cherry tomatoes in half. Place tomatoes on paper towels; sprinkle one side with curry powder and ½ teaspoon salt; flip and sprinkle the other side with remaining ½ teaspoon salt. Let stand 10 minutes.

4 Stir together mozzarella, cheddar, onion, mayonnaise, serrano, and red pepper in a large bowl. On a floured surface, roll pastry dough into a 12-inch circle or oval, trimming edges, if needed. Transfer dough to a parchment-paper-lined baking sheet. Spread cheese mixture over dough, leaving a 2½-inch border around edge. (You may not need all the cheese mixture.) Layer sliced tomatoes, curry side down, on cheese mixture; fill in with cherry tomatoes. Top with tamarind onions. Fold exposed border of dough circle toward center, pleating as necessary. Drizzle tomatoes and onions with olive oil; brush exposed crust with egg.

5 Bake in preheated oven until filling is bubbling and crust is golden brown, 20 to 25 minutes. Let cool 10 minutes. — *Samantha Fore*

WINE Pair with a cassis-scented Provençal rosé.

CHARRED SHISHITO PEPPERS
WITH GARLIC-HERB OIL

At Better Luck Tomorrow–his sleek Houston bar–**F&W** 2014 Best New Chef Justin Yu pairs blistered shishito peppers with a bright green, zesty garlic-herb oil that's a take on persil-lade, the French herb sauce. You'll want to keep this stuff around–it's fantastic drizzled on salads or tossed with hot pasta.

ACTIVE 40 MIN; TOTAL 1 HR; SERVES 8

MAKE THE GARLIC-HERB OIL

- 3 cups grapeseed oil
- 1 bunch fresh parsley (about 4 cups loosely packed)
- 1 bunch fresh cilantro (about 4 cups loosely packed)
- 10 fresh basil leaves
- 10 fresh mint leaves
- 4 garlic cloves
- 2 tsp. lime zest
- 2 tsp. Champagne vinegar
- 1 tsp. kosher salt
- ⅛ tsp. cayenne pepper

MAKE THE SHISHITO PEPPERS

- 1 lb. shishito peppers
- 2 Tbsp. grapeseed oil, canola oil, or other neutral oil
- 1 tsp. kosher salt
- 1 Tbsp., plus 1 tsp. fresh lime juice, for serving
- 1 tsp. flaked sea salt
- 1 tsp. lime zest

1 MAKE GARLIC-HERB OIL Set a large heatproof bowl in an ice bath.

2 Heat grapeseed oil in a large saucepan over medium until shimmering. Add parsley, cilantro, basil, mint, and garlic. Fry, stirring, until herbs are bright green and fragrant, about 15 seconds.

3 Working carefully and quickly, pour oil mixture into a blender. Process on low speed, gradually increasing speed to high until herbs are completely incorporated, about 2 minutes.

4 Pour the garlic-herb oil into prepared bowl for ice bath, and fold until mixture is chilled, about 1 minute. Add lime zest, vinegar, salt, and cayenne, and stir to combine. Chill garlic-herb oil until ready to serve.

5 MAKE THE SHISHITO PEPPERS Heat a 12-inch cast-iron skillet over high.. Toss peppers with oil and salt. Add half the peppers to pan. Cover and cook peppers until charred, about 8 minutes.

6 Uncover peppers and toss just until cooked through, about 10 seconds. Place cooked peppers in a bowl. Repeat procedure with remaining peppers. Dress warm peppers with 1 tablespoon lime juice and salt.

7 To serve, season garlic-herb oil with 1 teaspoon lime juice and transfer to a large shallow bowl set on a large serving platter. Arrange the shishito peppers around bowl for dipping, and sprinkle peppers with lime zest. —*Justin Yu*

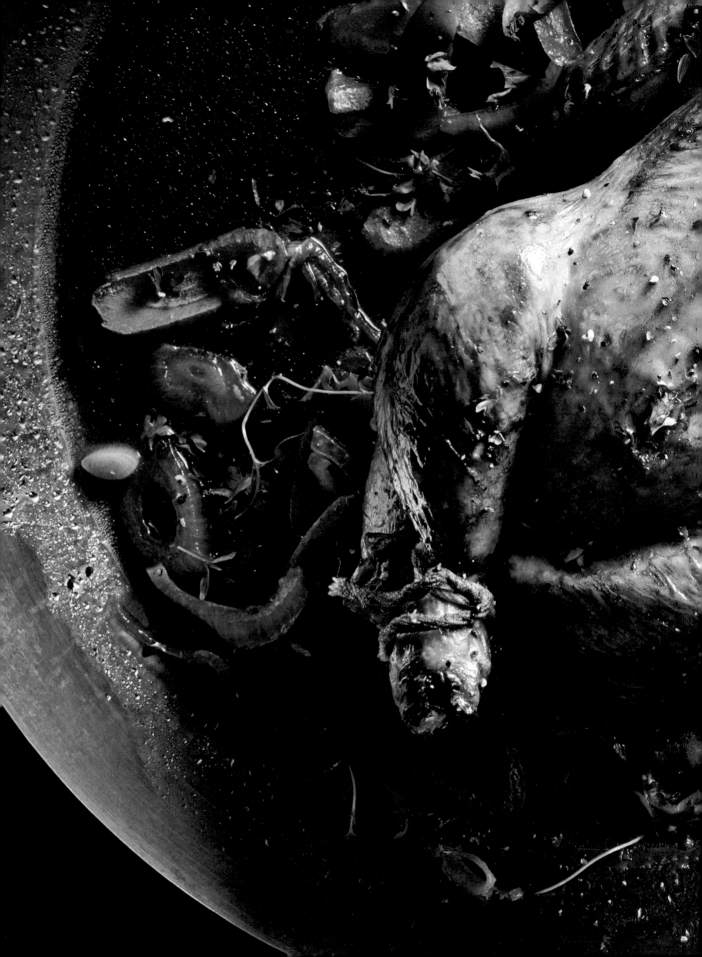

Meat & Poultry

GRILLED SKIRT STEAK
WITH CHIMICHURRI SAUCE

Chimichurri is now a common condiment, but this fresh and briny one from cookbook author and former *New York Times* food writer Mark Bittman was one of the first recipes we ran for it. It was so versatile and bright-tasting that it quickly became a staple condiment for many of us at **F&W**.

TOTAL 25 MIN; SERVES 8

2 cups chopped fresh parsley

⅔ cup extra-virgin olive oil

6 Tbsp. fresh lemon juice

2 Tbsp. minced garlic

2 tsp. crushed red pepper

Kosher salt

Freshly ground black pepper

4 lb. skirt steak

1 Preheat grill. Mix parsley, oil, lemon juice, garlic, and red pepper in a small bowl; season with salt and black pepper. Set sauce aside.

2 Season steak with salt and pepper, and grill until meat is charred on the outside and rare within, about 2 minutes per side. Transfer to a carving board and let rest for 5 minutes. Thinly slice steak across the grain. Serve right away, passing the chimichurri sauce at the table. —*Mark Bittman*

STEAK FRITES WITH BLACK GARLIC BUTTER

The keys to these crispy, curly frites from **F&W** senior food editor Mary-Frances Heck are first spiralizing them and then microwaving them until tender. The parcooked potatoes are flash-fried until crispy, making for the easiest homemade fries ever. For a next-level meal, spring for Charolais beef–a breed of cattle from Burgundy prized for its tender, flavorful, and marbled grass-fed meat. Source Charolais hanger steaks from Baldwin Beef or substitute a grass-fed or grass-finished hanger steak to channel the juicy, nutty qualities of the French beef.

TOTAL 1 HR 5 MIN; SERVES 4

1 head black garlic (see Note), peeled
¼ cup unsalted butter, softened
1 tsp. brandy
2¼ tsp. kosher salt, divided, plus more for sprinkling
2 lb. russet potatoes, spiralized into ¼-inch-thick strands
1 Tbsp. peanut or grapeseed oil, plus more for frying
1½ lb. trimmed Charolais hanger steaks or other grass-fed hanger steaks (2 to 3 steaks)
1 tsp. cracked black pepper
Finely chopped fresh flat-leaf parsley, for garnish (optional)

1. Place black garlic in a small bowl, and mash with a fork to a smooth paste. Add butter, brandy, and ¼ teaspoon salt; mash until thoroughly combined. Spoon garlic mixture onto a sheet of parchment paper or plastic wrap, and roll into a 3-inch-long log. Refrigerate until ready to use.

2. Mound spiralized potatoes on a large microwavable plate or in a glass pie plate; cover with wet paper towels. Microwave on high until tender, 4 to 6 minutes. Spread in an even layer on a rimmed baking sheet, and let cool 10 minutes.

3. Pour peanut oil to a depth of 1½ inches in a large, deep Dutch oven; heat over medium to 375°F. (The hot oil will rise when potatoes are added.)

4. Meanwhile, heat 1 tablespoon peanut oil in a 12-inch skillet over medium-high. Pat steaks dry with paper towels; sprinkle with pepper and remaining 2 teaspoons salt. Add steaks to skillet, and cook, turning every 3 minutes to evenly brown all sides, to desired degree of doneness, about 12 minutes for medium-rare. Transfer steaks to a carving board, and let rest 10 minutes.

5. Meanwhile, fry potatoes in hot oil in 2 to 3 batches, stirring often with a spider or slotted spoon, until frites are golden and crisp, 4 to 6 minutes. (Adjust heat between batches as needed to maintain oil temperature of 375°F.) Transfer frites to a butcher-paper-lined plate. Sprinkle with salt.

6. Slice steaks against the grain; divide among 4 plates. Cut black garlic butter into ½-inch-thick rounds. Top steak with black garlic butter and, if desired, parsley. Serve immediately with frites. — Mary-Frances Heck

MAKE AHEAD Black garlic butter may be stored in refrigerator up to 3 days or frozen up to 1 month.

NOTE Roasted garlic may be substituted for black garlic.

WINE Pair with a complex, structured red Burgundy.

GRILLED KOREAN-STYLE SHORT RIBS

Twenty years ago, way before Korean food was mega-trendy, Los Angeles food writers Linda Burum and Linda Merinoff were singing the praises of *kalbi*, the flanken-cut beef short ribs typical of Korean barbecue. The short ribs are marinated overnight in a simple mix of sake, soy, sugar, garlic, and sesame oil. Cooked quickly on a hot grill, the juicy meat is tender with a satisfying chew. The ribs make a stunning main course served alongside kimchi, lettuce leaves, and steamed rice. For the best results, ask your butcher to slice three or four ribs across the bone into ½-inch-thick pieces, and plan to marinate the meat overnight. The marinade is also delicious with chicken or pork.

ACTIVE 1 HR; TOTAL 9 HR 30 MIN; SERVES 10

- 5 lb. flanken-style (about ½-inch-thick) beef short ribs
- ⅓ cup sake
- ¼ cup granulated sugar
- 1 cup soy sauce
- 4 scallions (white parts and 2 inches of green parts only), finely chopped (about ⅓ cup)
- 7 large garlic cloves, finely chopped (about ¼ cup)
- 3 Tbsp. dark brown sugar
- ½ tsp. sesame oil
- 1⅓ cups water
- 2 Tbsp. vegetable oil
- ¼ tsp. black pepper

1 Place ribs in a large glass baking dish or enameled roasting pan; stir together sake and granulated sugar, and rub on both sides of ribs. Cover, and let stand 15 minutes.

2 Meanwhile, stir together soy sauce, scallions, garlic, brown sugar, and sesame oil in a medium bowl. Add 1⅓ cups water, and stir until sugar dissolves. Stir in vegetable oil and pepper. Pour soy mixture over ribs, and turn to coat evenly. Cover and refrigerate 8 hours or overnight. Return ribs to room temperature before cooking. Discard marinade.

3 Open bottom and top vents of a charcoal grill completely. Light a charcoal chimney starter filled with briquettes. When briquettes are covered with gray ash, pour onto bottom grate of grill and then push to one side of grill. Working in batches, place ribs on oiled grates directly over coals; grill, uncovered, until meat is seared, 1 to 2 minutes per side. Transfer ribs to side of grill without coals, and grill, uncovered, until tender, about 5 minutes per side. Remove from grill, and repeat procedure with remaining ribs. (If using gas grill, preheat only one side and, working in batches, cook ribs until tender.) —*Linda Burum and Linda Merinoff*

NOTE In lieu of grilling ribs, preheat broiler with oven rack 3 inches from heat; broil ribs until browned and ribs reach desired degree of doneness, 2 to 3 minutes per side for medium-well.

WINE Pair with a spicy, full-bodied California Zinfandel.

NACHO BURGERS

Of all the burger recipes *F&W* has run (more than 100), and of the six from chef Bobby Flay, this one is the over-the-top best, with juicy meat, gooey cheese, salsa, and tortilla chips. Need we say more?

TOTAL: 35 MIN; 4 SERVINGS

SALSA

- 3 plum tomatoes, finely diced
- 3 Tbsp. red wine vinegar
- 3 Tbsp. chopped fresh cilantro
- 2 Tbsp. red onion, finely diced
- 1 Tbsp. vegetable oil
- 1 chipotle chile in adobo, seeded and minced

  Kosher salt

CHEESE SAUCE

- 1 Tbsp. unsalted butter
- 1 Tbsp. all-purpose flour
- 1½ cups milk
- ½ lb. Monterey Jack cheese, shredded
- 2 Tbsp. freshly grated Pecorino cheese

  Kosher salt

  Freshly ground black pepper

BURGERS

- 1½ lb. ground beef chuck

  Vegetable oil, for brushing

  Kosher salt

  Freshly ground black pepper

- 4 hamburger buns, split and toasted

  Sliced pickled jalapeños and blue corn tortilla chips, for topping

1 MAKE THE SALSA Combine tomatoes, vinegar, cilantro, onion, oil, and chipotle chile in a medium bowl, and season with salt.

2 MAKE THE CHEESE SAUCE Melt butter in a small saucepan over medium. Stir in the flour, and cook for 30 seconds. Whisk in the milk, and cook, whisking, until smooth and thickened, 5 minutes. Stir in the Monterey Jack cheese until melted, then stir in the Pecorino; season with salt and pepper. Let the sauce cool until it is very thick and spreadable.

3 MAKE THE BURGERS Preheat grill to medium-high (about 450°F). Form the beef into 4 patties, and brush with oil; season with salt and pepper. Grill until browned outside and medium within, about 4 minutes per side.

4 Place the burgers on the buns. Top with the cheese sauce, salsa, jalapeños, and chips. Close the burgers and serve. —*Bobby Flay*

WINE Pair with a bold, berry-rich Zinfandel.

KOGI DOGS

Roy Choi was the first chef without a brick-and-mortar restaurant ever named a **F&W** Best New Chef (in 2010). His mission to bring great food to the streets via his Kogi Korean BBQ food truck represented a seismic shift in the way food was delivered and consumed around America. A Culinary Institute of America grad and former cook at Le Bernardin, he had a hard-core culinary pedigree, but the forward-thinking Korean native opted for a more unconventional path. When Kogi's first truck tweeted its stops, no one had ever heard of Korean short rib tacos. Soon, lines were endless, and smoky Kogi dogs, piled high with cabbage, kimchi, and cheddar, became a cult favorite.

TOTAL 40 MIN; SERVES 8

2 cups finely shredded cabbage

1 large scallion, finely chopped

1 Tbsp. fresh lime juice

Kosher salt

Freshly ground black pepper

1 Tbsp. toasted sesame seeds

½ cup mayonnaise

1 Tbsp. vegetable oil, plus more for brushing

1 cup kimchi, drained and patted dry

8 hot dog buns, split

8 all-beef hot dogs, partially split

4 oz. sharp cheddar cheese, shredded (about 1 cup)

2 cups shredded romaine lettuce

1 small onion, thinly sliced

2 cups cilantro sprigs

Sriracha chili sauce, for drizzling

1. Toss together cabbage, scallion, and lime juice in a large bowl; season with salt and pepper to taste. Using a mortar and pestle, crush the sesame seeds, and transfer to a small bowl. Stir in mayonnaise, and season with salt to taste.

2. Heat 1 tablespoon oil in a nonstick skillet over high. Add kimchi, and cook, stirring occasionally, until browned, about 3 minutes.

3. Preheat grill to medium-high (about 450°F). Brush cut sides of buns with oil, and grill, cut sides down, uncovered, until crisp, about 20 seconds. Flip and grill 20 seconds. Spread cut sides of toasted buns with sesame mayonnaise.

4. Grill hot dogs, uncovered, until nicely charred all over, about 3 minutes. Tuck hot dogs into buns, and top with kimchi and cheddar. Top hot dogs evenly with cabbage mixture, romaine, onion, and cilantro sprigs. Drizzle with Sriracha, and serve immediately. —*Roy Choi*

BEER Pair with a refreshing Mexican lager.

PIZZA WITH BAKED MEATBALLS

"'Avanzi' means 'leftovers,' in Italian," says Boston chef, cheesemaker, and James Beard nominee Matt Jennings, who often made this pizza on Fridays with his host family in Florence, using leftovers from the week of cooking. He urges people to get creative: "Char cucumbers and sprinkle feta on top. We've even put toasted ground nuts, dried fruit, and canned beans on the avanzi–although not necessarily at the same time!" We can't help but love a recipe that lends itself to this much versatility.

TOTAL 45 MIN; SERVES 4

1 Tbsp. extra-virgin olive oil, plus more for brushing

1 large egg

2 Tbsp. panko

2 garlic cloves, minced

¼ cup finely chopped fresh flat-leaf parsley

4 oz. Parmigiano-Reggiano cheese, grated (about 1 cup), divided

1 tsp. kosher salt

½ tsp. freshly ground black pepper

1 lb. ground beef chuck

1 (28-oz.) can crushed tomatoes

2 (8-oz.) balls of pizza dough, at room temperature

1 cup fresh basil leaves

1 Preheat oven to 450°F. Brush a large ceramic baking dish with oil. Whisk egg in a large bowl; stir in panko, garlic, parsley, ¼ cup cheese, 1 teaspoon salt, and ½ teaspoon pepper. Add ground beef, and gently knead to combine. Form mixture into 1-inch meatballs, and transfer to baking dish. Bake for about 10 minutes, turning once, until browned.

2 Meanwhile, heat 1 tablespoon oil in a large saucepan. Add crushed tomatoes, and cook over medium-high until bubbling.

3 Add meatballs to tomato sauce, cover partially, and simmer over medium-low until meatballs are cooked through, about 10 minutes. With a large spoon, mash meatballs into large chunks. Remove from heat.

4 Meanwhile, brush 2 large baking sheets with oil, and preheat in upper and lower thirds of oven. On a lightly floured work surface, cut each ball of dough in half. Roll each piece into a 10-inch oval. Arrange dough on heated baking sheets. Bake for about 7 minutes, shifting pans halfway through baking, until lightly golden on top.

5 Spread meatball sauce over crusts, leaving a ½-inch border around rims. Sprinkle with remaining ¾ cup cheese. Bake until crust is crisp on bottom and cheese is melted, about 5 minutes. Scatter basil leaves over pizzas and serve hot.
—*Matt Jennings*

TUSCAN-STYLE SPARERIBS
WITH BALSAMIC GLAZE

Chef Bruce Aidells is truly a master with meat, and these herb-and spice-rubbed spareribs are packed with flavor and perfect in texture. He generously seasons the ribs with a mix of aromatic herbs and spices and slow-roasts them until they're tender and crisp. Like his favorite Tuscan cooks do, he finishes the ribs with a simple balsamic glaze.

ACTIVE 20 MIN; TOTAL 4 HR 30 MIN; SERVES 6

- 2 Tbsp. extra-virgin olive oil
- 2 Tbsp. chopped fresh rosemary leaves
- 1½ Tbsp. kosher salt
- 1½ Tbsp. fennel seeds
- 2 tsp. freshly ground black pepper
- 2 tsp. chopped sage
- 2 tsp. chopped thyme
- 2 tsp. sweet paprika
- 1 tsp. crushed red pepper
- 1 tsp. ground coriander
- ½ tsp. ground allspice
- 6 lb. pork spareribs
- 3 Tbsp. balsamic vinegar, preferably one aged for at least 5 years

1 Combine oil, rosemary, salt, fennel, black pepper, sage, thyme, paprika, red pepper, coriander, and allspice in a small bowl. Rub spice paste all over spareribs, and let stand at room temperature for 2 hours or refrigerate overnight.

2 Preheat oven to 325°F. Arrange ribs on a large rimmed baking sheet or roasting pan, meaty side up. Roast ribs for 2 hours, or until tender.

3 Preheat broiler. Brush meaty side of ribs with vinegar, and broil 6 inches from heat until browned, about 2 minutes. Let stand for 5 minutes, then cut between the ribs and serve. —*Bruce Aidells*

WINE Pair with a slightly spicy medium-bodied red with low acidity or a lighter-bodied Sangiovese-based red like Chianti.

BRAISED SHORT RIBS

Flanken-style ribs (short ribs cut across the bones instead of parallel to them) become delightfully succulent when braised. This recipe from author and chef Tom Colicchio is just a great version of a classic red wine beef stew that you'll turn to over and again when you need some long-braised, soul-soothing food. Flanken-style short ribs can be ordered at butcher shops.

ACTIVE 1 HR; TOTAL 3 HR, PLUS 8 HR MARINATION; SERVES 6

- 2 Tbsp. canola oil
- 6 flanken-style beef short ribs with bones, cut 2 inches thick (about 4 lb.)
- Kosher salt
- Freshly ground black pepper
- 1 large onion, finely chopped
- 2 carrots, sliced
- 3 celery ribs, sliced
- 3 garlic cloves, thickly sliced
- 1 (750-ml) bottle dry red wine, such as Cabernet Sauvignon
- 4 thyme sprigs
- 3 cups chicken stock
- Mashed potatoes, buttered noodles, or crusty bread, for serving

1 Heat oil in a large skillet over medium. Season ribs with salt and pepper. Add ribs to skillet, and cook, turning once, until browned and crusty, about 18 minutes. Transfer ribs to a shallow baking dish in a single layer.

2 Add onion, carrots, celery, and garlic to skillet and cook over low, stirring occasionally, until very soft and lightly browned, about 20 minutes. Add wine and thyme sprigs and bring to a boil over high. Pour hot marinade over ribs, then let cool. Cover and refrigerate overnight, turning ribs once.

3 Preheat oven to 350°F. Transfer ribs and marinade to a large enameled cast-iron casserole. Add chicken stock and bring to a boil. Cover and cook in lower third of oven for 1½ hours, until meat is tender but not falling apart. Uncover and braise, turning ribs once or twice, until sauce is reduced by about half and meat is very tender, for 45 minutes longer.

4 Transfer meat to a clean shallow baking dish, discarding bones as they fall off. Strain sauce into a heatproof measuring cup and skim off as much fat as possible. Pour sauce over meat; there should be about 2 cups.

5 Preheat broiler. Broil meat, turning once or twice, until glazed and sizzling, about 10 minutes. Transfer meat to plates, spoon sauce on top, and serve with mashed potatoes, buttered noodles, or crusty bread. —Tom Colicchio

MAKE AHEAD. The braised short ribs can be prepared through Step 4 and refrigerated up to 2 days.

WINE Pair with a robust Spanish red.

TOM COLICCHIO

Tom Colicchio—named a *F&W* Best New Chef in 1991 and the winner of five James Beard Awards for both his restaurants and his cookbooks—never went to culinary school. It was a driving passion for cooking that spurred him to a life in food. His first kitchen job was at age 14 in the snack bar of the Gran Centurions Swim Club in Clark, New Jersey, making hamburgers and grilled cheese sandwiches. His mother, Beverly—who worked in the lunchroom of a public high school in his native Elizabeth, New Jersey—taught him to cook.

Study and experimentation in his home kitchen led him to New York City, where he cooked at such 1980s hot spots as The Quilted Giraffe, Gotham Bar & Grill, and Mondrian. In 1994, he and chef/partner, Danny Meyer, launched Manhattan's legendary New American restaurant, Gramercy Tavern.

While at Gramercy Tavern, he was asked what his favorite food was. The answer: morel mushrooms. It got him thinking, "Where can you go to eat just mushrooms or order a bowl of sweet, tender peas when they're at their best in early spring?"

He eventually left Gramercy Tavern and opened his flagship New York restaurant, Craft, in 2001. Today, the sprawling Craft empire features simply prepared dishes that celebrate pristine seasonal ingredients. Everything is served family-style, so guests can create their own plates.

Colicchio's interest in food goes beyond the aesthetic. In recent years he has become politically engaged in issues surrounding hunger and food insecurity in the United States. He has established himself as the top "Citizen Chef" fighting for a food system that puts access, affordability, and nutrition over corporate profits.

"As soon as one legislator loses their job over how they vote on food issues, we're going to send a clear message to Congress that we're organized and we're viable and we're strong," he told the *New York Times* in a 2014 interview. "We're going to make it clear that, yes, we do have a food movement—and that it's coming for you."

ZUCCHINI-AND-HERB-STUFFED CHICKEN

This recipe, first published in *Simple French Food*, was a favorite in the cooking classes of the late food writer and expatriate Richard Olney. To make it, flatten a spatchcocked chicken to an even thickness with a skillet, then stuff the zucchini-ricotta mixture under the loosened skin. The flavors and textures will only improve if you prepare the chicken up to Step 4 and refrigerate it uncovered on a rack overnight.

ACTIVE 40 MIN; TOTAL 2 HR SERVES 4 TO 6

2 lb. zucchini, grated

5½ tsp. kosher salt, divided

1 (3½-lb.) whole chicken, giblets removed

¾ cup ricotta cheese

¾ cup fresh breadcrumbs

2 oz. Parmigiano-Reggiano cheese, coarsely grated (about ½ cup)

¼ cup unsalted butter, softened

1 Tbsp. chopped fresh marjoram

1 large egg yolk

1 Tbsp. freshly ground black pepper, divided

2 Tbsp. herbes de Provence

2 Tbsp. extra-virgin olive oil

1 Toss together zucchini and 2 teaspoons salt in a colander set over a large bowl. Let stand until liquid is released, about 20 minutes. Transfer zucchini to a clean kitchen towel. Squeeze as much liquid from zucchini as possible.

2 While zucchini stands, pat chicken dry. Place chicken, breast side down, on a cutting board. Using poultry shears, cut along both sides of backbone; remove and discard backbone. Turn chicken breast side up. Place a heavy skillet on chicken breast, and press firmly against breastbone until it cracks and breast meat is an even 1-inch thickness. Transfer chicken to a wire rack in a large baking pan. Cut off wing tips at second joint; discard wing tips. Using your fingertips, gently loosen and lift skin from flesh of breasts, thighs, and drumsticks, being careful not to tear or totally detach skin. Set spatchcocked and prepped chicken aside.

3 Preheat oven to 425°F. Stir together ricotta, breadcrumbs, Parmigiano-Reggiano, softened butter, marjoram, egg yolk, drained zucchini, 1½ teaspoons salt, and 1½ teaspoons pepper until combined. Stuff zucchini mixture under skin of chicken breast, thighs, and drumsticks; carefully replace skin. Mold and evenly distribute stuffing, shaping and patting skin on outside of chicken.

4 Stir together herbes de Provence, remaining 2 teaspoons salt, and remaining 1½ teaspoons pepper in a small bowl. Drizzle oil over chicken, and sprinkle with herb mixture.

5 Bake chicken in preheated oven until skin is lightly browned, about 20 minutes. Reduce oven temperature to 325°F. Bake, basting after 30 minutes, until a meat thermometer inserted into thickest portion of thigh registers 155°F, about 50 minutes. Remove chicken from oven, and let rest until thermometer registers 165°F, about 20 more minutes. Carve chicken into 8 pieces, and serve. —*Richard Olney*

SIZZLING PANCAKES

In 1989, Binh Duong, a Vietnamese refugee who became a chef, owned one of the buzziest Vietnamese restaurants in America: Truc Orient Express in Hartford, Connecticut. Jacques Pépin was a fan. So was *F&W* Associate Test Kitchen Director Marcia Kiesel, who wrote that Duong's dishes had "a balance that appeals to the shyest or most cosmopolitan palate." Exhibit A: his bánh xèo, crisp and lacy rice crêpes colored with turmeric and studded with caramelized onions, shrimp, pork, and bean sprouts. The Vietnamese name of the dish translates to "sizzling cake"–so called for the sizzling sound the batter makes when it hits the pan. To cut the cook time in half, make two pancakes at once by using two skillets.

TOTAL 2 HR; SERVES 10

DIPPING SAUCE

- 2 red Thai chiles or 1 medium jalapeño, thickly sliced
- 2 medium garlic cloves, thickly sliced
- 2 Tbsp. granulated sugar
- 2 Tbsp. fish sauce
- 2 Tbsp. fresh lime juice
- 2 Tbsp. water

PANCAKES

- 2 cups rice flour (about 10½ oz.)
- 2¼ cups cold water
- 1 scallion, thinly sliced
- ¼ tsp. ground turmeric
- ¾ cup plus 3 Tbsp. vegetable oil, divided
- 1 lb. pork tenderloin, cut crosswise into very thin slices (about 30 slices), divided
- ½ lb. peeled and deveined raw medium shrimp (about 30 shrimp), divided
- 2 cups thinly sliced fresh shiitake mushroom caps, divided
- 1 cup thinly sliced yellow onion, divided
- 1¼ tsp. kosher salt, divided
- 1¼ tsp. black pepper, divided
- 2½ cups mung bean sprouts (about 7 oz.), divided

1 MAKE THE DIPPING SAUCE Pound chiles, garlic, and sugar with a mortar and pestle until mixture resembles a slurry, about 3 minutes. Stir in fish sauce, lime juice, and 2 tablespoons water until blended. Set aside.

2 MAKE THE PANCAKES Whisk together flour and 2¼ cups cold water in a medium bowl. Whisk in scallion and turmeric until blended. Set aside.

3 Preheat oven to 200°F. Heat 1½ tablespoons oil in a 10-inch nonstick skillet over high. Add 3 pork slices, 3 shrimp, and a few mushroom and onion slices. Sprinkle with ⅛ teaspoon salt and ⅛ teaspoon pepper. Cook until pork and vegetables are lightly browned, about 30 seconds per side.

4 Stir flour mixture. Remove skillet from heat. Holding skillet at an angle, pour in ⅓ cup flour mixture, and swirl to evenly coat bottom of skillet.

5 Return skillet to heat over medium. Cover and cook, undisturbed, until sides of pancake turn deep brown and curl up, about 5 minutes. Remove skillet from heat, and sprinkle ¼ cup bean sprouts over pancake. Fold in half, and transfer to a baking sheet; keep warm in preheated oven. Repeat procedure with remaining oil, pork, shrimp, mushrooms, onion, salt, pepper, and bean sprouts to make 9 more pancakes. Arrange pancakes on a large platter, and serve warm with dipping sauce. —*Binh Duong*

SABA-AND-DIJON-GLAZED EASTER HAM

As much as we respect tradition, we love when it gets tweaked (and even completely upended). This gorgeously glazed ham is a serious upgrade to an essential holiday staple. The chef-partner of Chicago's Monteverde restaurant, Sarah Grueneberg, switches up the traditional sugar-crusted ham by using saba, a sweet and slightly acidic syrup made from cooked-down grape must (similar to aged balsamic).

ACTIVE 20 MIN; TOTAL 1 HR, 25 MIN; SERVES 8 TO 10

1 lb. small carrots with tops, scrubbed and halved lengthwise

1 lb. shallots, peeled

¼ cup unsalted butter, divided

1 Tbsp. extra-virgin olive oil

2 tsp. kosher salt, divided

½ cup low-sodium chicken broth or water

½ cup plus 1 Tbsp. saba, divided

5 Tbsp. Dijon mustard, divided

1 (4- to 5-lb.) smoked spiral-cut ham

15 rosemary sprigs

1 Tbsp. sesame seeds, toasted

1 Tbsp. apple cider vinegar

1 Preheat oven to 400°F. Arrange carrots and shallots in an even layer in a large heavy roasting pan. Melt 2 tablespoons butter in a small skillet over medium. Drizzle melted butter and oil over vegetables, and sprinkle with 1 teaspoon salt. Roast in preheated oven until vegetables are slightly caramelized, about 20 minutes. Remove from oven and add broth to pan.

2 Whisk together ½ cup saba, 3 tablespoons Dijon, and remaining 1 teaspoon salt in a small bowl.

3 Place ham, bone side up, on a work surface. Nestle rosemary sprigs between slices, and place ham on top of vegetables in roasting pan.

4 Brush ham generously with one-third of saba mixture. Roast ham in preheated oven 5 minutes, and brush with half the remaining saba mixture. Reduce oven temperature to 250°F and roast ham until warmed through, about 25 minutes. Brush with remaining saba mixture, and increase oven temperature to 450°F. Roast until glaze is sizzling, about 5 minutes.

5 Place ham on a serving platter, and arrange vegetables around ham; tent with foil.

6 Heat pan drippings in a small saucepan over low. Stir in remaining 2 tablespoons Dijon, remaining 2 tablespoons butter, sesame seeds, and vinegar. Cook, stirring, until warmed through, about 5 minutes. Serve sauce with ham and vegetables.
—*Sarah Grueneberg*

PORK LOIN BRAISED WITH MUSHROOMS AND WINE

Aromatic Corsican Muscat wine, fresh herbs, fragrant strips of orange peel, and plenty of garlic perfume the braising liquid for this fabulous pork loin from Paris-based food writer Alexander Lobrano. The resulting jus is vibrant and richly seasoned; ladle extra over each serving of polenta.

ACTIVE 50 MIN; TOTAL 1 HR 20 MIN; SERVES 4

1 (2-lb.) boneless center-cut pork loin, tied with kitchen twine

1½ tsp. coarse sea salt

½ tsp. black pepper

3 Tbsp. olive oil

1 lb. white button mushrooms, quartered

8 small white spring onions (about 10 oz.), trimmed, white parts only

3 large garlic cloves, smashed

½ cup (4 oz.) Corsican Muscat wine

1 cup lower-sodium chicken stock

3 rosemary sprigs

6 thyme sprigs

8 (3-inch) orange peel strips

Cooked polenta, for serving

1 Preheat oven to 400°F. Sprinkle pork evenly with salt and pepper. Heat oil in a large ovenproof skillet or Dutch oven over medium-high.

2 Add pork to pan; cook over medium-high, undisturbed, until golden brown on one side, about 3 minutes. Turn pork. Repeat until each side is browned, about 12 minutes. Remove pork from skillet, and set aside.

3 Add mushrooms, onions, and garlic to pan; cook over medium-high, stirring often, until liquid from mushrooms has released and evaporated, about 8 minutes. Add wine; cook, scraping up browned bits from bottom of pan, until wine is reduced by half, about 5 minutes. Add stock, rosemary, and thyme; cook, undisturbed, 3 minutes. Return pork to pan. Cover, transfer to preheated oven, and roast until a thermometer inserted in thickest portion of meat registers 130°F, about 30 minutes.

4 Remove pan from oven. Transfer pork to a cutting board; let rest 5 minutes. Meanwhile, add orange peel strips to mushroom mixture in pan. Bring to a boil over medium-high; boil until sauce has slightly thickened, about 3 minutes. Discard orange peel strips, rosemary, and thyme.

5 Remove and discard twine from pork. Slice pork against the grain. Serve over polenta with mushroom mixture. — *Alexander Lobrano*

NOTE If you can't find Corsican Muscat, you can substitute Moscato d'Asti.

WINE Pair with an aromatic Corsican white.

MA PO TOFU

Quite simply, we think this updated version of the classic Sichuan dish *ma po tofu* from cookbook author Joyce Jue, which appeared in **F&W** in March 2002, is the tastiest tofu recipe we've come across. Even tofu naysayers admit to how good it is.

TOTAL 25 MIN; SERVES 4

- ¼ cup small tree ear mushrooms
- 2 Tbsp. soy sauce, divided
- 1 Tbsp. dry sherry or rice wine
- 1 tsp. Asian sesame oil
- 1 Tbsp. plus 1 tsp. cornstarch
- ½ lb. ground pork
- 1½ Tbsp. water
- 1½ Tbsp. vegetable oil
- 1 Tbsp. Chinese chili-bean sauce
- 2 garlic cloves, minced
- 2 tsp. minced fresh ginger
- 6 fresh water chestnuts, chopped
- 4 scallions, white and light green parts only, chopped
- ½ tsp. granulated sugar
- ¾ tsp. freshly ground white pepper
- 1 lb. firm tofu, drained and cut into ½-inch dice
- ¾ cup chicken stock or low-sodium broth
- ½ cup frozen baby peas, thawed

1 Place the mushrooms in a small bowl, and add water to cover; let soak for 15 minutes. Drain and coarsely chop.

2 Mix 1 tablespoon soy sauce with sherry, sesame oil, and 1 teaspoon cornstarch in a medium bowl; stir in pork. Mix remaining cornstarch with water in a small bowl.

3 Heat oil in a wok until smoking. Add chili-bean sauce, garlic, and ginger, and cook over high until fragrant, about 20 seconds. Add water chestnuts and chopped tree ears, and stir-fry for 15 seconds. Add pork, breaking up any large clumps, and stir-fry for 2 minutes. Stir in scallions, sugar, and pepper. Gently stir in tofu, broth, peas, and remaining 1 tablespoon of soy sauce, and bring to a boil. Add cornstarch mixture and stir until sauce thickens, about 15 seconds. Transfer to a platter and serve. —*Joyce Jue*

NOTE Ground pork isn't as widely available as ground beef, but it's easy to make at home. Dice inexpensive pork chops and pulse in the food processor until ground.

POACHED EGGS
WITH RED WINE SAUCE

In the early years, *F&W* had a distinctly French bent to it, especially in the recipes. Anne Willan, founder of the prestigious École de Cuisine La Varenne in France, expounded the virtues of cooking with red wine and shared a recipe for classic *oeufs pochés en meurette*, a Burgundian preparation reminiscent of eggs Benedict, with egg-topped buttered toast rounds. In her version, Willan used red Burgundy to make a rich, glossy sauce studded with bits of bacon, which she spooned over the runny eggs. She didn't insist on using Burgundian wine, but she strongly advised the cook: "If it is not fit to drink, it is not fit for the pot." Traditionally the eggs for this dish are poached in red wine; it adds a bit of flavor, but the eggs take on a grayish-purple color. This version calls for eggs that have been poached in water, then assembled with the red wine sauce at the end.

TOTAL 1 HR 30 MIN; SERVES 8

- 2 cups water
- ¼ cup veal demiglace
- 2 cups dry red wine (such as Burgundy)
- 1 cup chopped tomato
- 2 shallots, thinly sliced (about ¾ cup)
- Bouquet garni: 5 flat-leaf parsley sprigs, 1 thyme sprig, and 1 fresh bay leaf, tied securely with butcher's twine
- 1 (6-oz.) bacon slab, cut into ½-inch cubes (about 1¼ cups)
- 1 tsp. unsalted butter, softened
- 1 tsp. all-purpose flour
- ⅛ tsp. kosher salt
- ⅛ tsp. black pepper
- 8 poached eggs
- 8 white bread slices, cut into 3-inch rounds and sautéed in butter and oil until browned
- 2 Tbsp. finely chopped fresh flat-leaf parsley

1 Whisk together 2 cups water and demiglace in a large nonreactive saucepan over medium until demiglace dissolves, about 2 minutes. Stir in wine, tomato, shallots, and bouquet garni. Bring to a boil over high; reduce heat to medium-high, and simmer until reduced by half (about 2 cups), 50 to 55 minutes. Pour mixture through a fine wire-mesh strainer over a small nonreactive saucepan. Discard solids, and set wine mixture aside.

2 While wine mixture reduces, heat a medium skillet over medium-high. Add bacon, and cook, stirring often, until lightly browned, 5 to 6 minutes. Transfer to a paper-towel-lined plate to drain.

3 Stir together softened butter and flour in a small bowl until smooth to make a beurre manié. Bring reserved wine mixture to a simmer over medium, and gradually whisk in beurre manié. Cook, whisking constantly, until sauce is thick enough to coat the back of a spoon, 1 to 2 minutes. Remove from heat; stir in cooked bacon, and season with salt and pepper.

4 To serve, place 1 poached egg on each fried bread round; spoon about 2½ tablespoons wine sauce over each egg. Sprinkle evenly with parsley, and serve with remaining wine sauce. —*Anne Willan*

MAKE AHEAD This dish can be made up to 8 hours ahead. If you have poached the eggs ahead of time, cover with water and refrigerate them separately from the sauce. Before using the poached eggs, quickly immerse them in a large skillet of simmering water until just heated through, about 1 minute. Remove with a slotted spoon, and drain on paper towels. Wrap fried bread rounds loosely in foil and keep at room temperature.

LAMB CHOPS SIZZLED
WITH GARLIC

Journalist and cookbook author Janet Mendel has lived in and written about Spain for more than 40 years. Her fantastically garlicky lamb chops in their pan sauce of lemon, parsley, and crushed red pepper is her homage to the village of Las Pedroñeras, in the Castilla-La Mancha region, considered the garlic capital of Spain. This recipe's deliciousness defies its simplicity—and it takes just 20 minutes from start to finish.

TOTAL 20 MIN; SERVES 4

8 (½-inch-thick) lamb loin chops (about 2 lb.), fatty tips trimmed
Kosher salt
Freshly ground black pepper
Dried thyme
3 Tbsp. extra-virgin olive oil
10 small garlic cloves, halved
3 Tbsp. water
2 Tbsp. fresh lemon juice
2 Tbsp. minced fresh parsley
Pinch of crushed red pepper

1 Season lamb with salt and pepper, and sprinkle lightly with thyme. Heat oil in a very large skillet over medium-high until shimmering. Add lamb chops and garlic, and cook until chops are browned on bottom, about 3 minutes. Turn chops and garlic, and cook until chops are browned, about 2 minutes longer for medium doneness. Transfer chops to plates, leaving garlic in skillet.

2 Add 3 Tbsp. water, lemon juice, parsley, and red pepper to pan, and cook, scraping up browned bits from bottom of skillet, until sizzling, about 1 minute. Pour garlic and pan sauce over lamb chops and serve immediately. —*Janet Mendel*

GRILLED HERB LAMB
WITH FENNEL SAUCE

French cookbook author Madeleine Kamman preached the virtues of blending French technique with American ingredients in 1971, when she published her first book, *The Making of a Cook*. Kamman was a master at building and layering flavor, and this wonderful lamb exemplifies what made her so special.

ACTIVE 1 HR 15 MIN; TOTAL 3 HR 15 MIN; SERVES 6

1½ to 2 lb. boneless lamb rib rack, well trimmed

½ cup chopped fresh parsley

½ cup chopped fresh mint

½ cup chopped fresh basil

½ cup chopped fresh chives

1½ Tbsp. dried lavender flowers

3 garlic cloves, minced

6 Tbsp. unsalted butter, softened

½ tsp. kosher salt, divided

¼ tsp. freshly ground black pepper, divided

1½ Tbsp. vegetable oil

½ lb. lean lamb trimmings, obtained from the flaps of the back or well-trimmed boneless lamb stew meat, cut into 1-inch pieces

¼ tsp. fennel seeds

3 cups chicken stock or veal stock

Large bouquet of fresh herbs, for garnish

1 Using a small sharp knife, trim off any excess fat and the thin layer of silvery membrane that covers meat. Divide lamb where it begins to taper so the meat will cook evenly. If any piece is too long for your pan, cut it again.

2 Mix together parsley, mint, basil, chives, lavender, and garlic. Chop them together until finely minced. Sprinkle two-thirds of herb mixture over strips of meat, and press herb mixture into meat to help it adhere. Cover with plastic wrap, and let marinate for 2 hours at room temperature or up to 6 hours in the refrigerator. If you refrigerate meat, let it stand at room temperature at least 30 minutes before grilling.

3 Blend butter with remaining herb mixture. Season with ¼ teaspoon of salt and ⅛ teaspoon pepper. Using a large knife, scrape butter mixture onto plastic wrap, and roll into a 6-inch-long cylinder about 1½ inches in diameter. Place herb butter in freezer.

4 Heat oil in a medium-size heavy skillet over medium-high. Add lamb trimmings and sauté, stirring occasionally, until very well browned, about 10 minutes. Pour off any fat in pan. Add fennel seeds and stock. Bring to a boil, scraping up any browned bits from bottom of pan. Boil until stock is reduced to ⅔ cup of thick glaze, about 20 minutes. Strain into a small saucepan.

5 Preheat grill. Add lamb to grill, and brown on both sides, about 1½ minutes per side. Season meat with remaining ¼ teaspoon salt and ⅛ teaspoon pepper. Continue to grill, pressing down with a large spatula hard enough to flatten meat slightly in order to force heat to the center, for 3 to 4 minutes longer per side or until desired degree of doneness.

6 Place lamb on a carving board to rest. Meanwhile, cut herb butter into paper-thin slices, and arrange, overlapping, along center of each piece of meat.

7 Bring lamb glaze to a boil, and immediately pour a little over meat to begin melting butter. Cut meat crosswise on the diagonal into thin slices. Serve on warmed plates with remaining fennel sauce. Garnish with bouquet of fresh herbs.
—*Madeleine Kamman*

MAKE AHEAD This recipe can be prepared through Step 4 up to 6 hours in advance. Refrigerate fennel sauce; reheat before serving.

WINE Pair with a classic Bordeaux.

NOTE You'll need to special-order the boneless lamb rib rack from your butcher—they're not commonly available in most meat departments or butcher shops.

GARLICKY BRAISED LAMB
SHANKS WITH SWEET PEPPERS

Legendary chef Jeremiah Tower has been called the father of California cuisine, both as the chef at Chez Panisse in the 1970s, then at his own magnificent San Francisco restaurant, Stars, where this lamb shank dish was first served. Rich, mellow, saucy, and supremely satisfying, it was a dish that caught diners' eyes as it passed by their tables, inspiring them to immediately order it for themselves. At Stars, Tower served the shanks with an aioli flavored with rosemary and mint, but we like to devour them as they are. Chef Tower advises using a heavy Dutch oven just big enough to hold the shanks. The lamb can be braised a day ahead, making the meat extra tender and flavorful. The last-minute addition of fresh bell peppers injects a bright finish to the rich dish.

ACTIVE 1 HR 10 MIN; TOTAL 3 HR 10 MIN; SERVES 4

- 4 lamb foreshanks (about 5 lb.)
- 1¼ tsp. kosher salt, divided
- 1 tsp. black pepper, divided
- 2 Tbsp. unsalted butter, divided
- 12 unpeeled garlic cloves plus 24 peeled garlic cloves (from 4 heads), divided
- 6 fresh bay leaves
- 6 thyme sprigs
- 3½ cups low-sodium chicken stock
- 1 large red bell pepper, cut into ¼-inch strips
- 1 medium-size yellow bell pepper, cut into ¼-inch strips
- 1 Tbsp. fresh thyme leaves

1 Preheat oven to 300°F. Sprinkle lamb with 1 teaspoon salt and ½ teaspoon black pepper.

2 Heat 1 tablespoon butter in a large ovenproof Dutch oven over medium until foamy. Add 2 lamb shanks, all the unpeeled garlic cloves, bay leaves, and thyme sprigs, and cook, turning occasionally, until browned all over, about 15 minutes. Transfer browned shanks, unpeeled garlic, bay leaves, and thyme sprigs to a platter and set aside. Add remaining 2 lamb shanks to Dutch oven, and cook, turning occasionally, until browned all over, about 15 minutes. Return browned shanks, unpeeled garlic, bay leaves, and thyme sprigs to Dutch oven. Cover and transfer to preheated oven. Cook, flipping shanks every 20 minutes, until very tender, about 2 hours.

3 Remove lamb shanks, and set aside. Pour chicken stock into Dutch oven, and bring to a boil over high, scraping up any browned bits from bottom of Dutch oven. Remove from heat; use a ladle to skim off and discard fat from surface,. Return stock to a boil over high, skimming surface often and discarding fat, until reduced to 2 cups, about 10 minutes. Pour stock mixture through a fine wire-mesh strainer into a large measuring cup; discard solids. Skim remaining fat from surface, and discard. Wipe Dutch oven clean; pour strained stock into Dutch oven.

4 Add peeled garlic cloves to strained stock, and simmer over medium-low until garlic is slightly tender, about 20 minutes, flipping garlic cloves after 10 minutes. Return lamb to Dutch oven.

5 Scatter peppers and thyme leaves around lamb, and cook over medium-low, moving peppers around lamb occasionally, until peppers and garlic are tender, about 10 minutes. Using a slotted spoon, transfer lamb shanks to warm serving plates. Add remaining 1 tablespoon butter, remaining ¼ teaspoon salt, and remaining ½ teaspoon black pepper to sauce, and stir until creamy. Remove from heat. Spoon sauce with bell peppers and garlic cloves around lamb shanks.
—*Jeremiah Tower*

MAKE AHEAD The lamb can be cooked up to a day ahead. Refrigerate, covered; reheat before proceeding.

ROASTED VEAL CHOPS
WITH GRAPES

With just a handful of ingredients–most of them staples–and a simple method, this recipe from food writer and cookbook author Melissa Clark is so easy and yields a terrific result: beautifully crusted veal chops with grapes that cook down to an intensely fruity condiment. It's classic Melissa.

TOTAL 25 MIN; SERVES 4

1 lb. seedless red grapes

3 Tbsp. sherry vinegar

2½ Tbsp. unsalted butter, softened, divided

½ tsp. granulated sugar

Kosher salt

Freshly ground black pepper

4 (1-inch-thick) veal rib chops (about ½ lb. each)

1 Preheat oven to 500°F. Toss grapes, vinegar, 1½ tablespoons butter, and sugar on a sturdy rimmed baking sheet; season with salt and pepper. Roast, shaking baking sheet halfway through, until grapes are hot and pan is sizzling, about 10 minutes.

2 Rub veal chops with remaining 1 tablespoon butter, and season with salt and pepper. Push grapes to one side of baking sheet. Add veal chops, and roast until sizzling underneath, about 5 minutes. Turn chops, and roast until medium-rare, for 5 minutes longer. Transfer veal chops to a platter, scrape grapes and juices on top, and serve. —*Melissa Clark*

WINE Pair with a Super-Tuscan or rich Syrah.

JULIA'S FAVORITE ROAST CHICKEN

The little bit of extra treatment that this bird gets—with the brushing and basting with butter and lemon—makes it one of the best chickens ever. Julia Child seasoned it inside and out by packing sautéed vegetables, lemon slices, and fresh herbs into the cavity, then rubbing the skin with butter. In typical French fashion, she trussed the bird to promote even cooking.

ACTIVE 30 MIN; TOTAL 2 HR 15 MIN; SERVES 4

2½ Tbsp. unsalted butter, divided
⅓ cup finely diced carrots
⅓ cup finely diced onion
⅓ cup finely diced celery
1 tsp. thyme, savory, or mixed herbs, or 2 fresh thyme or savory sprigs
1 (3½- to 4-lb.) chicken
Kosher salt
Freshly ground black pepper
Parsley stems
Celery leaves
6 (⅛-inch-thick) lemon slices
½ cup sliced onion
½ cup sliced carrots
1 Tbsp. fresh lemon juice
¾ cup chicken stock or broth

1 Preheat oven to 425°F. Melt 1 tablespoon butter in a skillet. Add diced carrots, onion, and celery, and cook over medium until softened. Stir in thyme.

2 Wash chicken rapidly inside and out with hot water, and pat dry completely. For easier carving, cut out and discard wishbone. Pull neck skin up over breast, and secure it to back with a toothpick. Season the cavity with salt and pepper, and spoon in cooked vegetables, a handful of parsley stems, celery leaves, and lemon slices. Massage chicken all over with 1 tablespoon butter, then truss it. Alternatively, tie ends of drumsticks together and tuck wings under the body.

3 Choose a flameproof roasting pan that is about 1 inch larger than the chicken. Season chicken with salt, and set it breast up on a rack in pan.

4 Roast chicken in oven for about 1 hour and 15 minutes, as follows: At 15 minutes, brush chicken with remaining ½ tablespoon butter. Scatter sliced onion and carrots all around. Reduce oven temperature to 350°F. At 45 minutes, brush lemon juice over chicken. If necessary, add ½ cup of water to vegetables to prevent burning. At 60 minutes, baste with pan juices. Test for doneness: The drumsticks should move easily in their sockets; their flesh should feel somewhat soft. If not, continue roasting, basting, and testing every 7 to 8 minutes, until an instant-read thermometer registers 165°F.

5 Spear chicken through shoulders; lift to drain; if the last of the juices run clear yellow, chicken is done. Let rest on a carving board for 15 minutes; discard string.

6 Spoon all but 1 tablespoon of fat from juices in pan. Add stock, and boil until lightly syrupy, 5 minutes. Strain; you will have just enough to bathe each serving with a fragrant spoonful. —Julia Child

NOTE Throughout the process, thoroughly wash all surfaces and utensils that come into contact with raw chicken.

WINE Pair with a minerally, full-bodied Cour-Cheverny.

JULIA CHILD (1912–2004)

In the early 1960s, an unlikely advocate for French cooking burst onto the American scene. On the pages of *Mastering the Art of French Cooking* and in front of the camera on her groundbreaking PBS television show, *The French Chef*, Julia Child changed America's relationship to food with her contagious enthusiasm, wit, and candor.

In 1989, Child became a contributor to *F&W*. Her presence created considerable excitement. She was in her late seventies at that point, but one could argue she was only mid-career; she had published seven books and would go on to author or co-author 11 more. She invited us into her Cambridge, Massachusetts, home for a Christmas feature in 1993. For a Valentine's Day column in 1998, she shared the illustrated cards she and her husband, Paul, would send to friends.

While people usually associate Child with complex French dishes, many of her recipes for *F&W*, such as her roast chicken, weren't complicated at all. She always said that one can judge the quality of a cook by roast chicken, and that while it doesn't require years of training, it does entail "a greed for perfection." She often extolled the "forbidden delights of eggs and butter and fat and calories." Child warned against "fear of food," as she referred to it, insisting that some amount of fat was essential for good cooking, healthy brains and bodies, and joyful eating.

Bottom line, she felt that we'd all be happier if we ate well, treasured our meals, and cooked together. Countless times in the many years we worked with her, both before and after *F&W*, she'd turn to those around her in the kitchen and exclaim, "Isn't it so wonderful to cook with friends?"

POULET AU VINAIGRE

One of the world's most celebrated chefs and a leader of the French nouvelle cuisine movement, Paul Bocuse was an icon. Bocuse's irresistible chicken, cooked with vinegar, represented two big trends of the times: big, bold flavor and a focus on overall lightness, which Bocuse championed. With just a handful of ingredients and simple directions, this is a dish we have never stopped making. Paul Bocuse's take on chicken in vinegar sauce brightens and modernizes the classic French dish, swapping fresh tomatoes for tomato paste, using lower-acid rice wine vinegar in place of red wine vinegar, and significantly reducing the amount of butter.

TOTAL 1 HR; SERVES 4

- 3 Tbsp. clarified unsalted butter or 2 Tbsp. unsalted butter and 1 Tbsp. peanut oil
- 4 garlic cloves, unpeeled
- 1 (2½- to 3-lb.) whole chicken, cut into 10 pieces
  Kosher salt
  Freshly ground black pepper
- ½ cup mild white wine vinegar or rice vinegar
- ¾ lb. very ripe red tomatoes, peeled, cored, seeded, and cut into ¼-inch pieces (about 1½ cups)
- 2 Tbsp. chopped fresh flat-leaf parsley
- 2 Tbsp. unsalted butter

1 Preheat oven to 200°F. Heat clarified butter and garlic in a large heavy-bottomed skillet over medium-high. (The skillet should be large enough to hold all the chicken pieces in 1 layer.) Cook until the sound of sizzling butter has faded, about 3 minutes. Add chicken pieces, and cook until pieces are lightly browned, 5 to 7 minutes, flipping once after 3 minutes. Sprinkle generously with salt and pepper.

2 Add vinegar, and bring mixture to a rolling boil over medium-high; top chicken with tomatoes and parsley. Reduce heat to low; cover, and cook until chicken is cooked through, about 15 minutes, flipping chicken pieces after 7 minutes. Transfer chicken to a baking dish, and keep warm in preheated oven.

3 Using a spoon, skim and discard fat from surface of vinegar mixture in skillet. Continue to cook over low, undisturbed, until reduced by one-third, 3 to 4 minutes. Remove garlic cloves; peel cloves, and mash garlic pulp into sauce with a wooden spoon until blended. Add salt to taste. Whisk in 2 tablespoons butter until creamy.

4 Transfer chicken to a platter; pour sauce over chicken, and serve immediately.
—*Paul Bocuse*

NOTE To clarify butter, melt unsalted butter (any quantity you like—it keeps well in the refrigerator) in a saucepan over very low until clear. Remove pan from heat, and allow melted butter to stand for a few minutes until solids settle to bottom of pan. If there is any foam, skim it off with a spoon. Carefully pour off and reserve the clear liquid, which is clarified butter.

PORTUGUESE BRAISED PORK AND CLAMS

Smoked paprika is a little bit like magic dust. Just a touch adds amazing depth of flavor. For the best flavor in this simple braise of fresh clams and pork shoulder from *F&W* Executive Wine Editor Ray Isle, seek out a high-quality smoked paprika, such as Pimentón de la Vera dulce, which gets its sweet, rich, smoky flavor from being slowly dried over an oak fire.

ACTIVE 45 MIN; TOTAL 2 HR 50 MIN, PLUS 8 HR MARINATION; SERVES 8

- 2 lb. boneless pork shoulder, cut into 1½-inch cubes
- 2¾ tsp. kosher salt, divided
- ¾ tsp. black pepper, divided
- 6 garlic cloves, divided
- 1 cup dry white wine
- 2 bay leaves
- 1 Tbsp. Pimentón de la Vera dulce
- 1 Tbsp. extra-virgin olive oil, divided
- 1 medium yellow onion, thinly sliced
- 1 (28-oz.) can whole peeled tomatoes, drained and crushed by hand
- ½ tsp. crushed red pepper
- 2 cups chicken stock or low-sodium chicken broth, divided
- 2 lb. baby Yukon Gold potatoes, halved
- 2 lb. Manila clams or cockles, scrubbed

  Chopped fresh cilantro, for garnish

  Lemon wedges and crusty bread, for serving

1 Season pork all over with 1¼ teaspoons salt and ½ teaspoon black pepper, and place in a large resealable plastic bag. Smash 3 garlic cloves, and add to bag with wine, bay leaves, and Pimentón. Seal and refrigerate 8 hours or overnight.

2 Preheat oven to 350°F. Remove pork from marinade, and pat dry. Remove and discard garlic and bay leaves; reserve remaining marinade. Heat 1½ teaspoons oil in a large Dutch oven over medium-high. Add half the pork, and cook, stirring once or twice, until lightly browned, about 5 minutes. Transfer pork to a plate. Repeat with remaining pork. Chop remaining 3 garlic cloves, and add to Dutch oven with onion and remaining 1½ teaspoons oil; cook, stirring often, until golden, about 6 minutes. Stir in crushed tomatoes, red pepper, and reserved marinade.

3 Bring to a boil; reduce heat to medium-low, and simmer, stirring often, 3 minutes. Return cooked pork to Dutch oven; stir in 1 cup stock until pork is mostly submerged. Cover and bake in preheated oven until pork is fork-tender, 1 hour and 30 minutes to 2 hours.

4 Stir in potatoes and remaining 1 cup stock. Cover and bake until potatoes are tender, about 30 minutes.

5 Transfer Dutch oven to stovetop over high, and add clams. Cover and cook until clams open, 3 to 5 minutes. (Remove and discard any unopened clams.) Season with remaining 1½ teaspoons salt and remaining ¼ teaspoon black pepper. Garnish with cilantro. Serve with lemon wedges and crusty bread. — *Ray Isle*

MAKE AHEAD Pork may be prepared through Step 3 and refrigerated overnight. Reheat before proceeding with Step 4.

WINE Pair with a robust Portuguese red.

JERK CHICKEN

There are as many takes on jerk chicken in Jamaica as there are cooks on the island, but most share the same method: Chicken is first coated in a seasoning mixture dominated by spices and chiles, then grilled. This version comes from Paul Chung, a self-taught cook of Chinese-Jamaican descent who worked in the mail room at *F&W*. It's wonderfully spicy, smoky, and fragrant–everything you want jerk chicken to be. What puts this one above all others? The key is including Chinese five-spice in the marinade: "This spark of cinnamon enhances the rich clove flavor imparted by the allspice berries," *F&W* Test Kitchen Supervisor Marcia Kiesel wrote. For best results, let the chicken marinate overnight so the seasoning has time to thoroughly penetrate the meat. The chicken can also be roasted in the oven: Preheat oven to 500°F, and roast the chicken, skin side up, on the top rack.

ACTIVE 30 MIN; TOTAL 9 HR; SERVES 8

- 1 medium onion, coarsely chopped
- 3 medium scallions, chopped
- 2 Scotch bonnet chiles, chopped
- 2 garlic cloves, chopped
- 1 Tbsp. five-spice powder
- 1 Tbsp. allspice berries, coarsely ground
- 1 Tbsp. coarsely ground black pepper
- 1 tsp. dried thyme, crumbled
- 1 tsp. freshly grated nutmeg
- 1 tsp. kosher salt
- ½ cup soy sauce
- 1 Tbsp. vegetable oil
- 2 (3½- to 4-lb.) chickens, quartered

1 Combine onion, scallions, chiles, garlic, five-spice powder, allspice, pepper, thyme, nutmeg, and salt in a food processor. Process until mixture forms a coarse paste. With machine on, add soy sauce and oil in a steady stream. Transfer mixture to a large, shallow dish. Add chicken, and turn to coat. Cover and refrigerate overnight.

2 Bring chicken to room temperature. Preheat grill to medium-high (about 450°F). Place chicken on oiled grates; grill, uncovered, turning occasionally, until well browned and cooked through, 35 to 40 minutes. (Cover grill for a smokier flavor.) Transfer chicken to a platter, and serve. —*Paul Chung*

BEER Pair with a cold lager beer.

CARAMELIZED BLACK PEPPER CHICKEN

Working with chefs and their recipes has always been inspiring, from the most challenging dishes to the simple ones that become instant home classics. We asked Charles Phan, executive chef and owner of The Slanted Door in San Francisco, what he liked to cook at home, and he shared this take on caramelized black pepper chicken, a sweet and hot Vietnamese dish. It comes together in just minutes using ingredients that are common kitchen staples.

ACTIVE 25 MIN; TOTAL 35 MIN; SERVES 4

½ cup dark brown sugar

¼ cup fish sauce, or to taste

¼ cup water

3 Tbsp. rice vinegar

1 tsp. minced garlic

1 tsp. finely grated peeled fresh ginger

1 tsp. coarsely ground black pepper

2 fresh Thai chiles, halved, or dried red chiles

1 Tbsp. canola oil

1 shallot, thinly sliced

1 lb. skinless, boneless chicken thighs, cut into 1-inch pieces

4 cilantro sprigs

Steamed jasmine rice

1 Combine brown sugar, fish sauce, ¼ cup water, vinegar, garlic, ginger, pepper, and chiles in a small bowl.

2 Heat oil in a large, deep skillet over medium. Add shallot, and cook, stirring occasionally, until softened, about 4 minutes. Add sugar mixture and chicken, and simmer over high until chicken is cooked through, about 10 minutes. Transfer to a serving bowl. Garnish with cilantro, and serve with rice. —*Charles Phan*

WINE Pair with a ripe, oak-inflected California Chardonnay.

FRIED CHICKEN WITH TOMATO GRAVY AND THE BEST BISCUITS

Chef Scott Peacock met Edna Lewis when they cooked a fundraising dinner together in Georgia in 1990. The two shared a love for Southern cuisine and went on to forge a deep friendship, eventually publishing a book, *The Gift of Southern Cooking*. Taste and authenticity were paramount for both cooks, and this spectacular fried chicken speaks to that. Serve it with Lewis' light, fluffy, irresistible biscuits.

ACTIVE 1 HR 20 MIN; TOTAL 9 HR 20 MIN; SERVES 4

½ cup kosher salt

2 qt. cold water

1 (3½-lb.) whole chicken, cut into 8 pieces

3 cups buttermilk

1½ cups all-purpose flour (about 6⅜ oz.)

¼ cup cornstarch (about 1 oz.)

2 Tbsp. potato starch (optional)

1½ tsp. fine sea salt, plus more to taste

½ tsp. freshly ground black pepper, plus more to taste

1 lb. lard or vegetable shortening

½ cup unsalted butter (4 oz.)

¼ lb. bacon slices

1 small onion, finely chopped

1 garlic clove, minced

4 cups drained canned diced tomatoes (from 3 [14-oz.] cans)

2 tsp. dried thyme

2 cups heavy cream

1½ cups whole milk

The Best Biscuits (recipe follows)

1 Dissolve salt in 2 quarts of cold water in a large bowl. Add chicken; cover and chill 4 hours. Drain and rinse chicken. Place chicken in a large bowl. Add buttermilk, and turn pieces to coat. Cover and chill 4 hours.

2 Combine flour; cornstarch; potato starch, if using; 1½ teaspoons sea salt; and ½ teaspoon pepper in a gallon-size resealable plastic bag. Seal and shake. Set aside ½ cup seasoned flour for gravy. Remove chicken from buttermilk, wipe off excess, and place on a wire rack. Let dry 5 minutes. Add chicken, a few pieces at a time, to bag; seal and shake to coat. Shake off excess flour and return chicken to rack.

3 Melt lard and butter in a large cast-iron skillet over medium. Add bacon, and cook until crisp, about 5 minutes. Remove bacon, and reserve for another use. Working in batches if necessary, add chicken to bacon drippings, and cook, turning often, until golden, crisp, and cooked through, about 30 minutes. (Reduce heat if necessary.) Transfer fried chicken to a clean wire rack to drain.

4 Transfer ¼ cup pan drippings to a large saucepan. Add onion and garlic; cook over medium, stirring occasionally, until onion is golden, about 5 minutes. Add reserved ½ cup seasoned flour, and cook, whisking constantly, 2 minutes. Add tomatoes and thyme, and cook, stirring constantly, until blended. Whisk in cream and milk until smooth. Season with sea salt and pepper to taste, and cook, stirring occasionally, until thickened and no floury taste remains, about 10 minutes. Transfer fried chicken to a platter. Serve with gravy and The Best Biscuits. —*Scott Peacock*

THE BEST BISCUITS Preheat oven to 450°F. Sift together 1½ cups all-purpose flour, 1½ teaspoons baking powder, ¼ teaspoon baking soda, and ½ teaspoon kosher salt in a bowl. Using your fingers, work in ¼ cup cold lard or vegetable shortening, cut into pieces, just until mixture resembles coarse meal. Stir in ½ cup buttermilk just until moistened. Turn dough out onto a lightly floured work surface, and knead 2 or 3 times. Roll out or pat dough to ½-inch thickness. Using a 2-inch round cutter, stamp out biscuits as close together as possible. Transfer biscuits to a baking sheet. Pat dough scraps together, reroll, and cut out remaining biscuits (do not overwork dough). Pierce top of each biscuit 3 times with a fork, then brush biscuit tops with 1 tablespoon unsalted butter, melted. Bake in preheated oven until risen and golden, 12 to 14 minutes. —*Edna Lewis*

ZUNI ROAST CHICKEN AND BREAD SALAD

This roast chicken from chef Judy Rogers at San Francisco's Zuni Cafe is legendary, and it's only right to include it in the mix of the best recipes we ever published. Salting it for 24 hours and then roasting at a high temperature creates succulent meat and crispy skin.

ACTIVE 20 MIN; TOTAL 1 HR, PLUS 24 HR CHILLING; SERVES 4

1 (2¾-lb.) free-range chicken

4 thyme sprigs

4 small garlic cloves, lightly crushed and peeled

2 tsp. fine sea salt

Freshly ground black pepper

Bread Salad with Currants and Pine Nuts, for serving (recipe follows)

1 Using your fingers, gently loosen skin from chicken breasts and thighs. Stuff thyme and garlic under skin and spread in an even layer. Sprinkle salt all over chicken, and season with pepper. Cover and refrigerate at least 24 hours.

2 Preheat oven to 500°F. Preheat a large cast-iron skillet in oven for 5 minutes. Put chicken in skillet, breast side up, and roast for 30 minutes. Turn chicken breast side down, and roast about 15 minutes longer, or until juices run clear when a thigh is pierced. Transfer chicken to a board, and let rest for 10 minutes; carve.

3 Skim fat from juices in skillet. Arrange Bread Salad with Currants and Pine Nuts on a platter and top with chicken. Pour juices over all and serve. —*Judy Rogers*

BREAD SALAD WITH CURRANTS AND PINE NUTS Preheat oven to 450°F. Soak 1 tablespoon dried currants in 1 tablespoon red wine vinegar and 1 teaspoon warm water in a small bowl until plumped, 10 minutes. Drain. Combine 2 tablespoons Champagne vinegar, ½ cup extra-virgin olive oil, fine sea salt, and freshly ground black pepper to taste in another small bowl. Cut ½ pound stale Italian-style bread into large chunks. Toss with 2 tablespoons extra-virgin olive oil on a rimmed baking sheet. Bake about 5 minutes, until lightly toasted. Let cool, then tear bread into bite-size pieces. In a bowl, toss bread with three-quarters of the dressing, and let stand for 30 minutes. Meanwhile, in a pie plate, warm 1 tablespoon pine nuts in the oven for 2 minutes. Heat 1½ teaspoons extra-virgin olive oil in a skillet. Add 4 thinly sliced scallions and 3 thinly sliced garlic cloves, and cook over medium until softened, about 2 minutes; transfer to a large bowl. Add currants, bread, pine nuts, and remaining Champagne vinaigrette, and toss. Spoon bread salad into a shallow 1-quart baking dish. Cover loosely with foil, and bake about 15 minutes, until heated through. Uncover and bake a few minutes longer to dry top and bottom. Transfer bread salad to a platter, and toss with 4 cups lightly packed small arugula leaves.

WINE Pair with a ripe, rich Sonoma Chardonnay.

CHICKEN BIRYANI

Madhur Jaffrey brought India alive for us at *F&W*, as she did for all of her fans. In an article in 1990, she shared her technique for making perfect chicken biryani, a grand and festive casserole of rice layered with chicken. The key is keeping the rice grains separate (in India it is said that the grains of rice should be like two brothers: close, but not stuck together).

ACTIVE 1 HR; TOTAL 4 HR 35 MIN; SERVES 6

2 tsp. lightly packed saffron threads

3 Tbsp. hot milk

3 cups basmati rice, picked over

3 Tbsp. kosher salt, divided

1 (2-inch) piece of fresh ginger, peeled and coarsely chopped

5 garlic cloves

2 cups plain whole milk yogurt

½ cup coarsely chopped fresh mint

½ cup coarsely chopped fresh cilantro

1 to 2 fresh green chiles, thinly sliced

½ cup vegetable oil

3 medium onions, 2 halved lengthwise and thinly sliced, 1 finely chopped

¼ cup slivered almonds

¼ cup golden raisins

4 cinnamon sticks, divided

12 cardamom pods, divided

10 whole cloves, divided

2 fresh bay leaves, divided

1 tsp. black cumin seeds or ½ tsp. regular cumin seeds

6 chicken drumsticks, skin removed

6 chicken thighs, skin removed

2 Tbsp. fresh lemon juice

1 tsp. ground cumin

½ tsp. cayenne pepper

½ tsp. freshly ground black pepper

3 hard-cooked eggs, quartered

1 Heat a small cast-iron skillet over medium. When hot, add saffron, and stir until threads turn a few shades darker, about 1 minute. Pour hot milk into a small cup and crumble in the saffron threads. Set aside for 3 hours. Meanwhile, place rice in a large bowl, and wash in several changes of cold water. Add enough water to the bowl to cover rice by 2 inches. Stir in 1 teaspoon salt, and set aside to soak for at least 3 hours.

2 Combine ginger, garlic, and 1 tablespoon water in a blender. Blend on low-speed, scraping down sides a few times, until a fine paste forms.

3 Beat yogurt lightly in a bowl until smooth. Stir in mint, cilantro, and chiles.

4 Heat oil in a large, straight-sided skillet over medium-high. Add sliced onion, and cook, stirring once or twice, until deep reddish-brown and crisp, about 5 minutes. Using a slotted spoon, transfer onions to paper towels to drain. Reduce heat to medium. Add almonds to skillet, and cook, stirring constantly, until golden, about 30 seconds. Transfer almonds to paper towels to drain. Add raisins to skillet; they will plump up immediately. Quickly transfer them to paper towels to drain.

5 Add 2 cinnamon sticks, 6 cardamom pods, 5 cloves, and 1 bay leaf to skillet; Stir once and add cumin seeds. Stir once and add chopped onion. Increase heat to medium-high, and cook until onion is browned at the edges, about 1 minute. Add ginger-garlic paste, and stir-fry 1 minute. Add chicken pieces, and cook 1 minute. Add half the yogurt mixture, half the cooked almonds and raisins, 1½ teaspoons salt, lemon juice, ground cumin, and cayenne.

6 Stir ¼ cup water into skillet and bring to a simmer. Reduce heat to low. Cover and simmer gently for 10 minutes, then uncover and add half the cooked sliced onions. Increase heat to medium, and cook, stirring frequently, until sauce is dark and thickened and chicken is just tender, about 5 minutes. Add black pepper and salt to taste. Transfer chicken and sauce to a large ovenproof casserole.

7 Preheat oven to 375°F. Stir in ½ teaspoon salt and 2 teaspoons of reserved saffron milk into remaining yogurt. Spread mixture over chicken. In a Dutch oven, bring 10 cups water to a rolling boil. Add remaining 2 tablespoons salt, 2 cinnamon sticks, 6 cardamom pods, 5 cloves, and 1 bay leaf. Drain rice and slowly pour it into the pot. When water returns to a rapid boil, cook rice until just barely tender, 7 to 8 minutes; drain quickly, leaving in the spices.

8 Spoon rice over chicken in a heap. Working quickly, use a chopstick or a long spoon to make a well in center of rice to the bottom of the pot. Drizzle remaining saffron milk on sides of mound. Lay a clean, dampened cloth over rice and cover casserole tightly, first with a piece of foil and then with a lid. Bake for 35 minutes.

9 Stir rice gently with a slotted spoon, then spoon biryani onto a warmed platter. Garnish with remaining onions, almonds, raisins, and eggs. —*Madhur Jaffrey*

MAKE AHEAD This recipe can be prepared through Step 6 up to 6 hours in advance.

MADHUR JAFFREY

A touch of homesickness may have been responsible for introducing Americans to the glories of Indian food.

Jaffrey, an accomplished actress, writer, and television personality, left her native India in 1955 at the age of 22 to study at the Royal Academy of Dramatic Arts in London. The food at the school canteen—paper-thin slices of grey roast beef, mushy overcooked cabbage and watery potatoes—left much to be desired and Jaffrey dreaming of the tastes and aromas of her mother's cooking.

She wrote to her mother, who began sending her three-line recipes written in Hindi on onionskin paper. Jaffrey learned to prepare them as a student in London and, after she moved to New York in 1958 upon graduation, adapted the recipes for the ingredients she could get locally. The exercise in figuring out the details of the method from her mother's minimalist recipes would prove to be a valuable skill.

In 1966, *New York Times* food writer Craig Claiborne wrote an article about her, and the headline proclaimed, "Indian Actress Is a Star in the Kitchen, Too." The exposure led to her iconic 1973 *An Invitation to Indian Cooking*, which was inducted into the James Beard Foundation's Cookbook Hall of Fame in 2006. She has continued to champion the cuisine in numerous cookbooks and in several television shows.

Food writer Mayukh Sen has said of Jaffrey: "[She] was the first Indian cookbook author to really cut through the noise and challenge Americans to think beyond their misperceptions when it came to Indian food. She was the perfect translator for American home cooks in that era when they may have regarded Indian food with a sense of prejudice or stupefied curiosity. Madhur was also careful to root her writing in the personal rather than to make broad, overreaching statements about the cooking tra-

ROAST CHICKEN CACCIATORE
WITH RED WINE BUTTER SAUCE

Giada De Laurentiis is a chicken cacciatore expert: She's been making variations of it for years. For this exceptional version, the chef roasts a whole bird with red wine butter under the skin on a bed of fennel, cherry tomatoes, and Peppadew peppers. The red wine butter rubbed under the chicken skin ahead of roasting results in crazy-delicious meat.

ACTIVE 1 HR; TOTAL 2 HR 45 MIN; SERVES 4

- 1 (3½-lb.) chicken
- 3 tsp. kosher salt, divided, plus more to taste
- 5 thyme sprigs
- 1 cup red wine
- 2 Tbsp. tomato paste
- 2 Tbsp. unsalted butter, softened
- 4 basil sprigs, plus leaves for garnish
- 4 oregano sprigs
- 3 garlic cloves, crushed
- 1 small fennel bulb, cut into ¾-inch wedges through the core
- 1 cup cherry tomatoes
- ¾ cup pearl onions
- 8 jarred sweet Peppadew peppers, halved
- 6 baby bell peppers, halved lengthwise and seeded
- 1 Tbsp. extra-virgin olive oil
- ½ cup chicken stock
- ½ cup Castelvetrano olives, pitted and chopped

1 Season chicken with 2 teaspoons salt, and stuff thyme sprigs in cavity. Transfer chicken to a bowl, cover with plastic wrap, and poke holes in top; refrigerate overnight.

2 Boil wine in a saucepan over medium-high until reduced to 2 tablespoons, 7 minutes. Remove from heat; whisk in tomato paste, butter, and remaining 1 teaspoon salt. Let cool slightly.

3 Preheat oven to 400°F. Loosen breast and thigh skin of chicken, and spread three-fourths of the red wine butter under skin. Stuff basil sprigs, oregano sprigs, and garlic into cavity, and tie legs with string. Rub remaining red wine butter over chicken, and let stand for 30 minutes.

4 Meanwhile, toss fennel, tomatoes, onions, both peppers, and oil in a large, deep ovenproof skillet; season with salt. Set chicken in center of vegetables. Pour in stock. Roast 1 hour and 10 minutes, until an instant-read thermometer inserted in inner thigh registers 155°F. Transfer to a carving board, and let rest for 15 minutes.

5 Simmer broth over medium-high until slightly reduced, 3 minutes. Stir in olives, and transfer to a platter. Carve chicken, and arrange on platter. Garnish with basil leaves, and serve. —*Giada De Laurentiis*

WINE Pair with a Barbera.

CHICKEN TIKKA MASALA

Big-flavored, creamy, and comforting, chicken tikka masala is the perfect gateway dish to Indian cooking. This version, from former *F&W* Senior Test Kitchen Associate Grace Parisi, is relatively easy to prepare–and highly addictive, thanks to the slightly spicy tomato cream sauce. (For many years, this was the most popular recipe on foodandwine.com!) The chicken does need to marinate overnight, so plan accordingly.

ACTIVE 1 HR 35 MIN; TOTAL 9 HR 35 MIN; SERVES 4

MASALA MARINADE
- 1 cup plain low-fat yogurt
- 2 garlic cloves, minced
- 1 Tbsp. finely grated peeled fresh ginger
- 1½ tsp. ground cumin
- 1½ tsp. ground coriander
- ¼ tsp. ground cardamom
- ¼ tsp. cayenne pepper
- ¼ tsp. ground turmeric
- Kosher salt
- Freshly ground black pepper

CHICKEN
- 2½ lb. skinless, boneless chicken thighs, trimmed
- Kosher salt
- Freshly ground black pepper
- 2 Tbsp. plus 1 tsp. vegetable oil, divided
- ¼ cup blanched whole almonds
- 1 large onion, finely chopped
- 2 garlic cloves, minced
- 1 tsp. minced peeled fresh ginger
- 1½ Tbsp. garam masala
- 1½ tsp. pure chile powder
- ½ tsp. cayenne pepper
- 1 (28-oz.) can whole peeled tomatoes, finely chopped, juices reserved
- Pinch of granulated sugar
- 1 cup heavy cream

1 MAKE THE MASALA MARINADE Stir together yogurt, garlic, ginger, cumin, coriander, cardamom, cayenne, and turmeric in a large glass or stainless-steel bowl. Season with salt and black pepper.

2 MAKE THE CHICKEN Using a sharp knife, make a few shallow slashes in each thigh. Add chicken to marinade, and turn to coat. Cover, and chill 8 hours or overnight.

3 Preheat broiler with oven rack about 8 inches from heat. Remove chicken from marinade; discard marinade. Scrape off as much of the marinade from chicken as possible. Season chicken with salt and pepper, then spread in an even layer on a baking sheet. Broil chicken, flipping once or twice, just until cooked through and browned in spots, about 12 minutes. Transfer to a cutting board, and cut into 2-inch pieces.

4 While chicken broils, heat 1 teaspoon oil in a small skillet over medium. Add almonds, and cook, stirring constantly, until golden, about 5 minutes. Transfer almonds to a plate, and let cool completely. Place almonds in a food processor, and pulse until finely ground.

5 Heat remaining 2 tablespoons oil in a large Dutch oven over medium until shimmering. Add onion, garlic, and ginger, and cook, stirring occasionally, until tender, about 8 minutes. Add garam masala, chile powder, and cayenne, and cook, stirring constantly, 1 minute. Add tomatoes with their juices and sugar; season with salt and black pepper. Cover partially, and cook, stirring occasionally, until sauce is slightly thickened, about 20 minutes. Add cream and ground almonds; cook over low, stirring occasionally, until thickened, about 10 minutes. Stir in chicken; simmer gently, stirring often, for 10 minutes, and serve. —*Grace Parisi*

WINE Pair with a lemony Carneros Chardonnay.

Fish &
Shellfish

SEARED SALMON WITH SUMMER VEGETABLES

No one will contest that Union Square Cafe was one of the defining restaurants of the early '90s. Critics and diners were delighted by Danny Meyer's devout attention to hospitality and couldn't get enough of chef Michael Romano's remarkable Greenmarket-centric American-Italian food. Certain dishes defined the restaurant, including Romano's seared salmon, which was one of the most popular items on the menu and one of the best recipes we ever published. The myriad vegetables in the recipe–corn, spinach, shiitakes, and tomato–sing of late summer.

TOTAL 1 HR; SERVES 6

- ¾ cup unsalted butter (6 oz.), divided
- 1 cup thinly sliced red onion
- 3 garlic cloves, 2 thinly sliced and 1 whole, divided
- ¼ lb. shiitake mushrooms, stems removed and reserved, caps quartered, divided
- 1 medium-size ripe tomato, coarsely chopped
- 1 tsp. whole black peppercorns
- 1 fresh bay leaf
- ⅓ cup balsamic vinegar
- ⅓ cup water
  Kosher salt
  Freshly ground black pepper
- 3 Tbsp. extra-virgin olive oil, divided
- 1 lb. fresh spinach
- 2 cups fresh corn kernels
- 1 (1-lb.) center-cut salmon fillet, sliced crosswise into 6 strips
- 3 Tbsp. finely chopped chives

1 Cut 6 tablespoons butter into ½-inch cubes, and refrigerate until ready to use. Melt 2 tablespoons butter in a medium nonreactive saucepan over medium-low. Add onion, sliced garlic cloves, shiitake stems, tomato, black peppercorns, and bay leaf, and cook until vegetables are soft but not brown, about 12 minutes. Add vinegar and ⅓ cup water; increase heat to medium-high, and cook, stirring occasionally, until mixture is syrupy, about 4 minutes.

2 Reduce heat to low, and add cubed butter, 2 or 3 pieces at a time, whisking thoroughly between additions. Season sauce with salt and pepper to taste. Pour sauce through a fine wire-mesh strainer into a bowl; discard solids. Keep sauce warm over a double boiler.

3 Spear whole garlic clove with a dinner fork. Heat 2 tablespoons oil in a large skillet over high until just beginning to smoke. Add spinach; cook, stirring using fork with garlic clove, until spinach is wilted. Season with salt and pepper to taste; transfer to a colander to drain. Discard garlic clove.

4 Wipe skillet clean with paper towels. Reduce heat to medium, and add 3 tablespoons butter. Add shiitake caps, and cook, stirring, until softened, about 3 minutes. Stir in corn kernels; cook until completely heated through, about 3 minutes. Season with salt and pepper to taste. Transfer to a bowl, and keep warm.

5 Increase heat to high, and add remaining 1 tablespoon butter and remaining 1 tablespoon oil to skillet. Season salmon strips with salt and pepper to taste. Add fish to skillet, and cook until browned but barely cooked through, about 3 minutes per side.

6 Divide spinach among 6 plates; surround with corn and shiitakes. Place a salmon strip on top of spinach, and spoon vinegar sauce on fish. Garnish with a sprinkling of chives; serve immediately. —*Michael Romano*

WINE Pair with a Chenin Blanc, Rioja Blanco, strong Pinot Noir, or medium-weight Bordeaux.

PAN-ROASTED SALMON WITH TOMATO VINAIGRETTE

Whenever a recipe is tested at *F&W*, the team gathers round to sample and discuss it. This unassuming salmon didn't really grab anyone's attention while it sat on the table, but once it was tasted, everyone paused and quieted. It was disarmingly simple but perfect. To make it, Ted Allen, TV personality and host of Food Network's *Chopped*, sautéed sweet grape tomatoes with capers, shallot, and cumin, then spooned the bright, chunky sauce over crisp salmon fillets. It's easy and quick and makes the quintessential weeknight dinner.

TOTAL 30 MIN; SERVES 4

1 pt. grape tomatoes, halved
1 medium shallot, thinly sliced
2 Tbsp. red wine vinegar
1 Tbsp. drained capers
½ tsp. kosher salt, plus more
3 Tbsp. extra-virgin olive oil, divided
4 (7-oz.) skin-on center-cut salmon fillets
   Freshly ground black pepper
2 Tbsp. canola oil
½ tsp. ground cumin
1 Tbsp. minced fresh flat-leaf parsley
1 Tbsp. chopped fresh basil

1 Preheat oven to 425°F. Toss together tomatoes, shallot, vinegar, capers, and ½ teaspoon salt in medium bowl.

2 Heat 1 tablespoon olive oil in a medium ovenproof skillet over medium-high. Season salmon with salt and pepper. Place fillets in skillet, skin sides up. Cook until well-browned on bottom, about 3 minutes. Carefully flip fillets. Transfer skillet to preheated oven, and roast until salmon is cooked through, about 7 minutes. Divide fillets among 4 plates, and discard any fat in skillet.

3 Return skillet to heat over medium, and add tomato mixture, remaining 2 tablespoons olive oil, canola oil, and cumin. Cook, stirring to scrape up any bits stuck to bottom of skillet, just until tomatoes soften, about 2 minutes. Top salmon with sauce, and sprinkle with parsley and basil. —*Ted Allen*

WINE Pair with a strawberry-scented Malbec rosé.

PIZZA WITH SMOKED SALMON, CRÈME FRAÎCHE, AND CAVIAR

Wolfgang Puck's insanely popular "designer" pies at Los Angeles' Spago pioneered an anything-goes approach to toppings. One of his very first avant-garde creations, made with silky smoked salmon, crème fraîche, and caviar, changed pizza forever. In his original recipe, Puck called for black or golden caviar to top this delectable pizza. Today, sustainable, affordable caviar, like farmed sturgeon or salmon roe, makes Puck's game-changing dish even easier to make at home.

ACTIVE 40 MIN; TOTAL 8 HR; MAKES 2 (8-INCH) PIZZAS

1 cup lukewarm water

½ tsp. active dry yeast

2¾ cups type-0 flour, plus more for dusting

3 Tbsp. extra-virgin olive oil, divided, plus more for greasing

1¼ tsp. kosher salt

2 Tbsp. chopped fresh chives, divided

6 Tbsp. crème fraîche

4 oz. thinly sliced smoked salmon

¼ cup black or golden caviar (about 2 oz.)

1 Whisk together 1 cup lukewarm water and yeast in a large bowl; let stand until foamy, about 5 minutes. Add flour, 1 tablespoon oil, and salt, and stir until a dough forms. Scrape onto a lightly floured work surface, and knead until smooth, about 5 minutes. Transfer to a large greased bowl. Cover with plastic wrap, and let stand in a warm place 1 hour.

2 Cut dough in half, and shape into 2 balls. Transfer balls to 2 large greased bowls. Cover with plastic wrap, and let stand in a warm place until doubled in size, about 5 hours.

3 Preheat oven to 500°F. Place a pizza stone in the oven, and heat 30 minutes.

4 Punch dough balls down. Press ½ teaspoon chives into each dough ball. On a lightly floured work surface, roll each ball into an 8-inch circle. Brush each dough circle with 1 tablespoon oil, leaving a 1-inch border. Transfer dough circles to a lightly floured pizza peel or the back of a baking sheet dusted with flour. Slide dough circles onto hot pizza stone, and bake until golden brown, 8 to 10 minutes.

5 Spread each pizza crust evenly with 3 tablespoons crème fraîche, and top each with 2 ounces smoked salmon. Place 2 tablespoons caviar in the center of each pizza, garnish with remaining 5 teaspoons chives, and serve immediately.
—*Wolfgang Puck*

MAKE AHEAD The dough can be refrigerated overnight or frozen up to 1 month. Let it come to room temperature before using.

WINE Pair with a lightly herbal New Zealand Sauvignon Blanc.

WOLFGANG PUCK

When Wolfgang Puck arrived in California in 1975 after working in Michelin three-star restaurants—such as Maxim's in Paris—he wanted to surf and ride a dune buggy. "Instead," he says, "I worked all the time."

It didn't take long for him to make his name in Los Angeles at the French institution Ma Maison. In 1982, when he opened Spago on a hillside above the Sunset Strip, it could not have been predicted it would launch a dining revolution.

At the time, with its unobstructed dining room and open kitchen, there was no doubt about whose hands were cooking the house-made duck sausage or white asparagus—two of the hallmarks of the playful but meticulously prepared menu that helped make California the most famous food state in the country.

If he did not invent all the innovations credited to Spago, he probably did more than anyone to popularize them: the warm salads, the wood-fired designer pizzas, the shift from classical French to casual Italian—daring ideas now solidly in the mainstream.

The wunderkind of California cuisine is now the patriarch of America's first epicurean empire. He controls 14 restaurants, has more than 80 Wolfgang Puck Gourmet Express locations in 23 states, and produces frozen pizza, canned soup, and estate-grown coffee. He hawks his own line of cookware and appliances on the Home Shopping Network and runs catering venues from Los Angeles Staples Center to the Georgia Aquarium. He employs some 4,500 workers, and last year, he fed an estimated 10 million people.

"When I was 30, I thought, if I'm not retired by 55, I'll shoot myself," he says. "But I'm not ready—80 would be a good time to slow down a bit."

BAKED FLOUNDER WITH PARMESAN CRUMBS

There really isn't much work or fuss in this delicious fish from chef and author Nigel Slater, which is why we liked it so much. It's so satisfying when a handful of accessible ingredients comes together to make something that's just right.

ACTIVE 10 MIN; TOTAL 30 MIN; SERVES 4

4 flounder fillets (2 lb. total)
Kosher salt
Freshly ground black pepper
2½ oz. Parmesan, grated (about ¾ cup)
½ cup coarse fresh breadcrumbs
4 Tbsp. unsalted butter, melted
2 Tbsp. extra-virgin olive oil

Preheat oven to 425°F. Season fish with salt and pepper in a large baking dish. Mix Parmesan, breadcrumbs, butter, and oil in a small bowl; sprinkle over fish. Bake until fish is cooked and topping is golden, 15 minutes. Let stand for 5 minutes before serving. *—Nigel Slater*

NOTE To get ½ cup of coarse fresh breadcrumbs, place 1½ slices of crusty bread in a food processor and process until coarsely crumbled.

BLACK COD WITH MISO

We'd only really ever had sable smoked, so when we tried this, it was a complete "ah-ha" moment, as it has been for hoards of Nobu fans! Who knew cod could be so good? With just a few ingredients, this black cod from chef Nobu Matsuhisa is one of the silkiest, most luxurious pieces of fish imaginable. Nobu marinates the black cod in a good deal of the sake-miso marinade for two to three days, but the fish is also spectacular if you marinate it only overnight in just enough sake and miso to coat.

TOTAL 30 MIN PLUS OVERNIGHT; SERVES 6

- 3 Tbsp. mirin
- 3 Tbsp. sake
- ½ cup white miso paste
- ⅓ cup granulated sugar
- 6 (6- to 7-oz.) skinless black cod fillets, about 1½ inches thick
  Vegetable oil, for brushing
  Pickled ginger, for serving

1 Combine mirin and sake in a small saucepan; bring to a boil. Whisk in miso until dissolved. Add sugar, and cook over medium, whisking, just until dissolved. Transfer marinade to a large baking dish, and let cool. Add fish, and turn to coat. Cover and refrigerate overnight.

2 Preheat oven to 400°F. Heat a grill pan and oil it. Scrape marinade off fish. Add fish to pan, and cook over high until browned, about 2 minutes. Flip fish onto a heavy rimmed baking sheet and roast until flaky, 10 minutes. Transfer to plates and serve with pickled ginger. *—Nobu Matsuhisa*

MAKE AHEAD The marinade can be refrigerated up to 1 week.

SNAPPER IN CHILE-LIME SAUCE

Cooking whole fish doesn't get much easier or more delicious than this. Inspired by a dish she had in Mexico's coastal Veracruz region, chef Zarela Martinez, of the now-shuttered Zarela in New York City, quickly fries red snapper, then cooks it in a tangy, fresh, and vivid tomatillo salsa. The salsa is fabulous on this crispy snapper, but it would be equally wonderful on simple grilled chicken, steak, or shrimp.

TOTAL 40 MIN; SERVES 4

½ lb. tomatillos, husks removed
1 tsp. kosher salt, plus more
½ cup fresh lime juice
½ small onion, coarsely chopped
4 jalapeños, seeded and chopped
4 cilantro sprigs
3 garlic cloves
¼ cup water
½ cup pure olive oil
1 (2-lb.) red snapper, cleaned
2 Tbsp. unsalted butter

1 Place tomatillos in a small saucepan; sprinkle with a pinch of salt. Cover with water; bring to a boil, and cook just until tomatillos change color, 5 minutes. Drain and let cool. Transfer tomatillos to a blender; add lime juice, onion, jalapeños, cilantro sprigs, garlic cloves, and ¼ cup of water; and puree until blended.

2 Heat oil in a large nonstick skillet. Season fish inside and out with 1 teaspoon of salt. Add fish to skillet, and cook over medium-high, turning once, until golden and crisp, 15 minutes.

3 Tilt pan slightly and spoon off oil. Add sauce, and cook, spooning sauce over fish, until it is hot and fish is cooked through, 5 minutes. Using 2 spatulas, transfer fish to a platter. Add butter to skillet; swirl until melted. Season sauce with salt, pour over fish, and serve. —Zarela Martinez

WINE Pair with a lively, citrusy Sauvignon Blanc.

FISH TACOS WITH CREAMY LIME GUACAMOLE

These fish tacos from the late Rock 'n' Roll Chef Kerry Simon are the epitome of the perfect healthy fish taco, with none of the fattiness of traditional fried fish tacos. The crunchy cabbage slaw is a must and easily stands on its own as a side dish to an array of simple grilled dishes.

TOTAL 45 MIN; SERVES 10

- 2 Hass avocados, halved, pitted, and peeled
- ¼ cup low-fat sour cream or Greek yogurt
- 1 small jalapeño, seeded and thinly sliced
- 2 Tbsp. minced red onion
- 2 Tbsp. chopped fresh cilantro
- 5 Tbsp. fresh lime juice, divided

  Kosher salt

  Freshly ground black pepper
- 1 small head napa cabbage, shredded (4 cups)
- 2 Tbsp. vegetable oil, plus more for brushing
- 2 lb. thick red snapper fillets with skin, cut crosswise into ten 2-inch-wide strips
- 10 (7-inch) flour tortillas, warmed
- 2 medium tomatoes, thinly sliced

  Hot sauce, for serving

  Lime wedges, for serving

1 Preheat grill to medium-high (about 450°F). Mash avocados in a medium bowl, and mix in sour cream, jalapeño, onion, cilantro, and 3 tablespoons lime juice. Season guacamole with salt and pepper, and press a piece of plastic wrap directly onto the surface of guacamole.

2 Toss cabbage with 2 tablespoons oil and remaining 2 tablespoons lime juice in a large bowl. Season with salt and pepper.

3 Brush fish with oil, and season with salt and pepper. Grill until lightly charred and cooked through, about 10 minutes. Transfer fish to a platter, and pull off skin.

4 To assemble each taco, spread a dollop of guacamole on a tortilla. Top with a piece of fish, a few tomato slices, and a large spoonful of cabbage slaw. Serve with hot sauce and lime wedges. —*Kerry Simon*

WINE Pair with a coastal California Chardonnay.

SWORDFISH SICILIAN-STYLE

The late legendary cookbook author Marcella Hazan joined *F&W* as a contributing editor in 1992. Former Executive Food Editor Tina Ujlaki remembers that although technique mattered to Hazan, "taste trumped all." Of all the wonderful recipes she created, our all-time favorite is this quick-cooking swordfish, where an oregano-infused sauce imparts bright flavor to hot-off-the-grill steaks. The secret is pricking holes in the fish so the lemony dressing seeps in.

TOTAL 20 MIN; SERVES 4 TO 6

- 2 Tbsp. fresh lemon juice
- 2 tsp. kosher salt
- 2 tsp. chopped fresh oregano or 1 tsp. dried oregano
- ¼ cup extra-virgin olive oil
  Freshly ground black pepper
- 2 lb. ½-inch-thick swordfish steaks

1 Preheat grill to high (450°F to 550°F), or preheat broiler. Stir together lemon juice and salt in a small bowl until salt dissolves. Stir in oregano. Slowly whisk in oil, and season generously with pepper.

2 Place swordfish steaks on oiled grill grates; grill, uncovered, until cooked through, about 3 minutes per side.

3 Transfer fish to a platter. Using a fork, pierce fish in several places. Using a spoon, beat oil mixture, and drizzle it over fish. Serve immediately. —*Marcella Hazan*

WINE Pair with a focused, lightly herbal Etna white.

MARCELLA HAZAN
(1924–2013)

Marcella Hazan was an amazing, intuitive home cook. This may sound like a simplistic description of the woman who introduced Americans to her native cuisine more than 35 years ago with *The Classic Italian Cookbook*. But we were lucky to have spent time in Hazan's kitchen and to work on her stories for *F&W* through the years. Cooking at home for her husband, Victor, and their family and friends is what made her recipes so easy for home cooks to follow.

For the Hazans, flavor always came first. We would occasionally try to talk them out of dishes that we knew would be a challenge to photograph—like bean soups or whole roasted veal shanks that resembled nuclear reactor towers—but they always won. We sometimes questioned the simplicity of a recipe, but many favorites, like her legendary roast chicken with two lemons and tomato sauce with butter, have fewer than five ingredients.

When Hazan came to New York from Emilia-Romagna as a newlywed in 1955, she didn't know how to cook. She'd earned a doctorate in natural sciences and biology from the University of Ferrara—her training was in the classroom, not the kitchen. But like so many who uproot themselves and settle in a new place, missing the flavors of home is powerful impetus to re-create them. She started learning to cook by using cookbooks from Italy but soon discovered she had an inherent understanding of how to reproduce those flavor memories. Before long, she was giving cooking lessons in her apartment and opened her own cooking school—The School of Classic Italian Cooking—in 1969.

Fellow Italian food personality Lidia Bastianich said of Hazan in her *New York Times* obituary, "She was the first mother of Italian cooking in America."

SWORDFISH COOKED WITH FRESH GREEN CHUTNEY

When Madhur Jaffrey wrote her first book, *An Invitation to Indian Cooking* (Knopf, 1973), Indian flavors were exotic to Americans. In fact, when this recipe was published, fresh chiles and cilantro were hard to track down. More than 45 years later, this spicy and fragrant fish still stands out as one of our favorites.

TOTAL 40 MIN; SERVES 6

CHUTNEY

- ½ cup chopped fresh Chinese parsley, well packed with no stems
- 1 fresh hot green chile, sliced
- 3 cloves garlic, peeled
- 4 Tbsp. fresh lemon juice
- ¼ cup water
- ½ tsp. kosher salt
- 1 tsp. ground cumin seeds
- 2 tsp. granulated sugar
- 1½ cups fresh grated coconut

SWORDFISH

- 3 lb. swordfish, cut into 1-inch-thick slices
- Freshly ground black pepper
- 6 Tbsp. unsalted butter, cut into 12 pieces
- Fresh lemon wedges and chopped parsley, for garnish

1 MAKE THE CHUTNEY Combine parsley, green chile, garlic, lemon juice, and water in a food processor and process until smooth. Transfer mixture to a mixing bowl, and stir in salt, cumin, sugar, and coconut.

2 MAKE THE SWORDFISH Using a long, sharp knife, divide swordfish into six portions. Season lightly with salt and pepper. On a large work space, cut six squares of aluminum foil, each measuring 10- × 12-inches. Divide chutney into 12 portions. Place a pat of butter in the center of each foil square, then top with one portion of chutney. Spread chutney on foil to the approximate size of one piece of fish. Top chutney with a piece of fish, and cover with another portion of chutney. Top with another pat of butter. Fold edges of foil over fish and seal.

3 Preheat grill. Arrange fish packets on grill, and cook for 10 minutes per side or until fish is done. Serve fish with lemon wedges and chopped parsley.
—*Madhur Jaffrey*

CRISPY CRAB CAKES
WITH TOMATO BUTTER

Patrick Clark's crab cakes at Tavern on the Green were legendary, taking on a pop of flavor from chopped fresh jalapeño and a crispy exterior from panko. Chopped whitefish provides the structure in these crab cakes, offering more flavor and a richer texture than traditional binders like breadcrumbs. Look for plastic tubs, rather than cans, of jumbo lump crabmeat; it's fresh and unpasteurized, with the cleanest taste and best texture. If whitefish is unavailable, substitute sea bass or cod.

ACTIVE 1 HR; TOTAL 1 HR 10 MIN; SERVES 4

- 4 oz. skinless whitefish fillet
- 3 jalapeños, seeded, 1 finely diced, divided
- ½ cup mayonnaise
- ⅓ cup thinly sliced scallions
- 1 Tbsp. chopped fresh flat-leaf parsley
- 2 tsp. kosher salt, divided
- 1 tsp. black pepper, divided
- ½ tsp. cayenne pepper
- 1 lb. fresh jumbo lump crabmeat, drained and picked over
- 1½ cups panko
- 6 small plum tomatoes (about 1 lb.), cored and halved
- 3 medium shallots, chopped
- 3 medium garlic cloves, chopped
- 6 Tbsp. olive oil, divided
- 2 cups chicken stock
- ¼ cup unsalted butter, cut into pieces
- 2 cups mixed fresh summer herbs (such as basil, mint, and flat-leaf parsley)
- 1 lemon, cut into 4 wedges, for serving

1 Preheat oven to 450°F. Place whitefish in a food processor, and process until mostly smooth; transfer to a large bowl. Add diced jalapeño; stir in mayonnaise, scallions, parsley, 1 teaspoon salt, ½ teaspoon black pepper, and cayenne. Gently fold in crabmeat, leaving lumps intact. Divide mixture into 8 portions (about ⅓ cup each); shape into 3-inch-wide, ½-inch-thick patties. Sprinkle both sides of patties generously with panko to coat completely; press lightly to adhere. Refrigerate 30 minutes.

2 While patties chill, stir together tomatoes, shallots, garlic, 1 tablespoon oil, and remaining 2 jalapeños in an ovenproof skillet. Roast in preheated oven until tomatoes collapse, about 15 minutes. Remove skillet from oven, and transfer to stovetop over medium. Add stock, and cook, stirring often, until most of the liquid has evaporated and mixture is reduced to about 1½ cups, about 15 minutes. Transfer mixture to a blender. Secure lid on blender, then remove center piece to allow steam to escape. Place a clean towel over opening. Process, gradually adding butter pieces through opening, until mixture is smooth and butter is combined. Season with ½ teaspoon salt and ¼ teaspoon black pepper; keep sauce warm.

3 Heat ¼ cup oil in a large skillet over medium-high. Working in batches, cook crab cakes until golden brown, 2 to 3 minutes per side. Transfer to a wire rack to cool.

4 Toss herbs with remaining 1 tablespoon olive oil, remaining ½ teaspoon salt, and remaining ¼ teaspoon pepper. Spread about ⅓ cup sauce on each of 4 plates; top evenly with herb salad and crab cakes. Serve with lemon wedges. — *Patrick Clark*

WINE Pair with a bright, chalky Chablis.

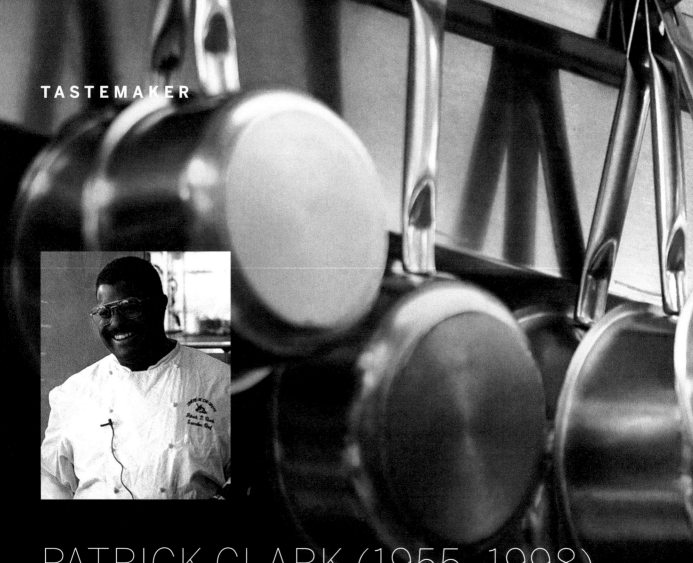

PATRICK CLARK (1955–1998)

Patrick Clark was the executive chef at the groundbreaking New American restaurant The Odeon in New York at age 25 and a James Beard Award winner—a first for a black chef—at 39, for his tenure at the Hay-Adams Hotel in Washington, D.C.

Brooklyn-born-and-raised, he was a classically trained powerhouse and one of the leaders of New American cooking in the late '80s and '90s, after studying under Michel Guérard in France. There he learned *cuisine minceur*—focusing on healthy approaches to French dishes—and applied this sensibility to the menu at The Odeon.

In February of 1998, Clark died at age 42 while waiting for a heart transplant. The chef community put together a cookbook to raise money for his wife, Lynette, and their five children. It included warm remembrances and recipes from a host of his peers—Thomas Keller, Jacques Pépin, Alice Waters, and Daniel Boulud among them. Marcus Samuelsson wrote, "As a young chef arriving in New York, I frequently looked to Patrick for guidance and inspiration. Being the most famous and respected black chef in the U.S. was a huge responsibility for him, and one he gladly accepted. As a role model and leader, Patrick opened many doors for young, aspiring chefs who otherwise would not have chosen this industry."

At the 2018 James Beard Awards, Edouardo Jordan became the first black chef to win the Best New Restaurant accolade for his Seattle restaurant, JuneBaby. He thanked Clark in his acceptance speech.

"There should be a Patrick Clark Day," he said. "He paved the way for a lot of us. I'm constantly asking myself if he would be proud of me."

STIR-FRIED SHRIMP WITH
BACON, MINT, AND CHILES

This singular stir-fry from James Beard Award-winning Seattle chef Jerry Traunfeld is a magical combo of sweet shrimp, salty bacon, hot chiles and vermouth, showered with fresh mint at the end.

TOTAL 25 MIN; SERVES 4

- 2 tsp. vegetable oil
- ¼ lb. thickly sliced bacon, cut crosswise ¼ inch thick
- 3 garlic cloves, minced
- 8 Thai bird chiles or 4 serrano chiles
- 1½ lb. shelled and deveined raw large shrimp
  Kosher salt
  Freshly ground black pepper
- ¼ cup vermouth or dry white wine
- ¼ cup plus 2 Tbsp. coarsely chopped fresh mint

Heat oil in a large skillet over medium. Add bacon, and cook, stirring occasionally, until most of the fat has been rendered. Spoon off all but 1 tablespoon fat from skillet. Stir in garlic and whole chiles, and cook until fragrant, about 1 minute. Add shrimp; season with salt and pepper, and cook over high, stirring occasionally, until pink and curled, about 3 minutes. Add vermouth, and cook until nearly evaporated, about 1 minute. Stir in mint, transfer to plates, and serve. —*Jerry Traunfeld*

WINE Pair with an aromatic, faintly sweet Riesling.

SHRIMP CREOLE

Before he was a television food megastar, Emeril Lagasse made a name for himself in the '80s as the chef at the legendary Commander's Palace in New Orleans, arguably the city's best restaurant at the time. Lagasse was a master of "haute Creole" cooking, a complex blend of Creole and Cajun with signature dishes such as baked redfish en papillote and bread pudding soufflé. (The soufflé is still on the Commander's Palace menu today.) On a visit to New York City in 1984, Lagasse visited the *F&W* Test Kitchen and shared several recipes, including his shrimp creole, a dish that stands proudly on its own when served over steamed rice, but which Lagasse used as an accompaniment to chicken-and-shrimp jambalaya.

TOTAL 45 MIN; SERVES 4

2 Tbsp. unsalted butter

1 medium yellow onion, chopped

1 medium green bell pepper, chopped

2 celery stalks, chopped

5 garlic cloves, finely chopped

1¼ cups chicken stock or canned chicken broth

4 tsp. Creole Seafood Seasoning (recipe follows) or more to taste, divided

1 tsp. hot paprika

⅛ tsp. cayenne pepper

4 fresh bay leaves

2 cups coarsely chopped tomatoes

3 scallions, chopped

1 Tbsp. Worcestershire sauce

1 tsp. Louisiana-style hot sauce

½ tsp. kosher salt

2 Tbsp. vegetable oil

1½ lb. peeled and deveined raw medium shrimp

1 Melt butter in a large skillet over medium-high. Add onion, bell pepper, celery, and garlic. Cook, stirring occasionally, until vegetables are softened but not browned, 5 to 7 minutes.

2 Add chicken stock, 2 teaspoons Creole seasoning, paprika, cayenne, and bay leaves. Bring to a boil over high; reduce heat to medium, and simmer until slightly reduced, about 5 minutes. Stir in tomatoes, and cook, stirring occasionally, until slightly thickened, about 10 minutes.

3 Stir in scallions, Worcestershire sauce, hot sauce, and salt; cook, stirring often, until thick but still a little saucy, about 10 minutes. Set aside Creole sauce.

4 Heat oil in a large skillet over medium-high; swirl to coat. Add shrimp; sprinkle with remaining 2 teaspoons Creole seasoning (or to taste), and cook, stirring often, until slightly pink, about 1 minute.

5 Add Creole sauce to shrimp; cook, stirring, until shrimp are pink, cooked through, and coated in sauce, 3 to 4 minutes. —*Emeril Lagasse*

CREOLE SEAFOOD SEASONING Combine ⅓ cup kosher salt, ⅓ cup paprika (preferably hot), ¼ cup freshly ground black pepper, ¼ cup garlic powder, 3 Tbsp. onion powder or dried minced onion, 2 Tbsp. cayenne pepper, 2 Tbsp. dried thyme, and 2 Tbsp. dried oregano in a food processor, and pulse until well combined, about 1 minute.

MAKE AHEAD The Creole sauce can be made through Step 4 and chilled up to 4 days or frozen for up to a month.

Pasta & Grains

PASTA WITH SAUSAGE, MUSTARD, AND BASIL

In matching spicy sausage with a creamy mustard sauce and fragrant basil, British cookbook author Nigel Slater created a quick-cooking, spectacularly satisfying, and quintessentially English supper. This quick and tasty pasta is the perfect meal for a cool fall or winter evening.

TOTAL 20 MIN; SERVES 4

Kosher salt

1 lb. dried penne or medium shell pasta

1 Tbsp. extra-virgin olive oil

8 hot Italian sausages (about 1½ lb.), meat removed from casings and crumbled

¾ cup dry white wine

¾ cup heavy cream

3 Tbsp. grainy mustard

Pinch of crushed red pepper

1 cup thinly sliced fresh basil

1 Bring a large pot of salted water to a boil. Add pasta, and cook according to package directions for al dente; drain.

2 Heat oil in a large deep skillet over medium-high. Add sausage; cook until browned, about 5 minutes. Add wine; simmer, scraping up browned bits from bottom of skillet, until reduced by half, about 5 minutes. Add cream, mustard, and red pepper; simmer 2 minutes. Remove from heat. Add pasta and basil, then toss.
—*Nigel Slater*

WINE Pair with a full-bodied, plummy Washington Merlot.

CREAMY LEMON PASTA

Chef and TV personality Andrew Zimmern mimics the sweet, fragrant lemons of Italy's Amalfi Coast with Meyer lemons in this beautifully bright and creamy pasta. The dish originated at L'Antica Trattoria in Sorrento, where lemon juice is tossed with just-cooked pasta until absorbed. Supremes of lemon add a juicy, tart pop that cuts through the cream in the sauce.

ACTIVE 15 MIN; TOTAL 20 MIN; SERVES 4

- 4 qt. water
- 2 Tbsp. plus ¾ tsp. kosher salt
- ¾ cup extra-virgin olive oil
- 1 Tbsp. lemon zest, from Meyer lemon
- 1 tsp. honey
- 3 medium shallots, minced (about ½ cup)
- 1 cup heavy cream
- 1 lb. dried fettuccine
- 2 Tbsp. fresh lemon juice, from Meyer lemon
- 3 oz. grated Parmigiano-Reggiano cheese (about ¾ cup)
- ½ tsp. freshly ground black pepper, for garnish
- ⅓ cup lemon supremes, from Meyer lemon, for garnish

1 Bring 4 quarts water to a rapid boil in a large pot, and season with 2 tablespoons kosher salt.

2 Meanwhile, heat oil and lemon zest in a large skillet over medium. Add remaining ¾ teaspoon salt, honey, and shallots, and cook until shallots are softened and oil is hot, about 5 minutes. Whisk in cream. Let simmer 2 minutes.

3 Cook pasta in the boiling water until al dente. Reserve ½ cup cooking liquid; drain. Add lemon juice to noodles; toss well to combine. The pasta will absorb the juice.

4 Stir cheese and ¼ cup reserved cooking liquid into skillet with cream sauce. Add pasta, and toss to coat well. Add remaining ¼ cup reserved cooking liquid, if necessary. Divide among 4 bowls, and garnish with pepper and Meyer lemon supremes. — *Andrew Zimmern*

WINE Pair with a bright, citrusy Campanian white.

PASTA PRIMAVERA

We love what's happening in the world of pasta in recent years. If the standard boxed stuff is your go-to for easy weeknight dinners, it's time to take your game to the next level. Artisanal dried pastas are now common on grocery store shelves and are well worth the switch. Extruded through bronze dies, they have a rough, textured surface that helps sauces cling to the pasta. This pasta dish from *F&W* recipe developer Liz Mervosh is buttery and rich but still feels light from the lemon zest and fresh herbs–it's the perfect dish to make after a visit to your local farmers' market. The colorful play of spring vegetables makes it as pleasing to the eyes as it is to your palate. If you're lucky enough to find beautiful red or purple carrots, add them after cooking to keep from giving your pasta dish a blushing hue.

TOTAL 35 MIN; SERVES 4

- 1 lb. fresh asparagus (medium to thick stalks), trimmed
- 6 oz. small multicolor carrots (about 12 carrots)
- 12 oz. dried bronze-cut durum wheat tagliatelle pasta
- 12 Tbsp. cold unsalted butter (6 oz.), cut into ½-inch pieces, divided
- 1 Tbsp. finely chopped garlic (from 3 medium garlic cloves)
- ¼ cup water
- ¼ tsp. kosher salt
- 4 oz. fresh sugar snap peas, trimmed and thinly sliced lengthwise (about 1 cup)
- 1 cup fresh pea shoots, plus more for garnish
- ¾ oz. Parmigiano-Reggiano cheese, grated (about ½ cup), plus more for garnish
- 2 Tbsp. chopped fresh chives
- 2 tsp. chopped fresh tarragon
- 1 tsp. lemon zest plus 2 tsp. fresh lemon juice (from 1 lemon)

1 Using a Y-shape vegetable peeler, shave asparagus into very thin ribbons to equal 1 cup. Shave the purple carrots (from multicolor carrots) into very thin ribbons to equal ½ cup. Shave remaining carrots into very thin ribbons to equal ½ cup. (Reserve remaining asparagus and carrots for another use.) Set aside.

2 Cook pasta in a pot according to master technique (until very al dente, about 3 minutes shorter than package directions call for).

3 While pasta cooks, place purple carrot ribbons in a fine wire-mesh strainer. Lower strainer into boiling water with pasta, and cook carrots until tender, about 20 seconds. Remove strainer; drain carrots, and set aside. Melt 1 tablespoon butter in a large skillet over medium. Add garlic; cook, stirring often, until fragrant, about 1 minute. Add ¼ cup water; let come to a simmer. Gradually whisk in 5 tablespoons butter, one piece at a time, waiting until butter is nearly melted before adding the next piece. Stir in salt.

4 Using tongs, lift cooked pasta from pot, and transfer to skillet, reserving cooking liquid in pot. Increase heat under skillet to medium-high. Add snap peas, asparagus ribbons, uncooked carrot ribbons (do not add purple carrot ribbons), and remaining 6 tablespoons butter; cook, stirring and shaking skillet constantly, adding ¼ cup reserved cooking liquid at a time, until a creamy sauce forms and clings to pasta, 2 to 3 minutes.

5 Remove skillet from heat. Add pea shoots, cheese, chives, tarragon, and lemon zest and juice, stirring constantly until thoroughly combined and cheese is melted. (Add a little more cooking liquid if necessary to maintain a creamy consistency.)

6 Divide pasta mixture among 4 bowls. Top evenly with purple carrot ribbons; garnish with additional pea shoots and cheese. — *Liz Mervosh*

WINE Pair with a crisp, citrusy Italian Vermentino.

RIGATONI WITH LEMONY KALE PESTO

Kale began to be ubiquitous in the early 2010s and shows no sign of waning in popularity. We thought we'd seen it every which way—sautéed, steamed, braised, baked into crispy chips, and even grilled—when we came came across this recipe from San Francisco chef Chris Cosentino. Using it in a pesto was a first for us! It also was an excellent way to make a winter version of pesto.

TOTAL 30 MIN; SERVES 4 TO 6

1½ lb. Tuscan kale, stemmed

1 lb. dried rigatoni

3 large garlic cloves

¼ cup pine nuts, toasted

⅔ cup extra-virgin olive oil

1½ oz. Pecorino Toscano cheese, coarsely grated (½ cup), plus more for serving

1 Tbsp. finely grated lemon zest (from 1 lemon)

Pinch of Aleppo pepper, plus more for seasoning

Kosher salt

Freshly ground black pepper

1 Bring 2 large pots of generously salted water to a boil. Fill a large bowl with ice water. Add kale to one of the pots, and cook until bright green and just tender, 1 minute. Drain and immediately transfer to ice water. When cool, drain again. Transfer kale, with water clinging to leaves, to a work surface, then chop.

2 Meanwhile, add rigatoni to the other pot of boiling water. Cook until almost al dente. Reserve ½ cup cooking water, then drain pasta.

3 Transfer kale to a blender. Add garlic and pine nuts, and pulse until coarsely chopped. Add oil and process until smooth. Transfer pesto to a large bowl, and stir in ½ cup Pecorino and lemon zest. Season to taste with Aleppo pepper, salt, and black pepper.

4 Return pasta to pot. Add pesto, and cook over medium, stirring constantly, for 2 minutes, adding some of the pasta water if it seems dry. Spoon pasta into bowls, top with additional cheese and Aleppo pepper, and serve. —*Chris Cosentino*

CACIO E PEPE PASTA PIE

We've done a lot of fairly classic mac and cheese recipes, so this "pie" from *F&W* Culinary Director Justin Chapple popped out for us. It's hard not to love for its presentation, and with its crispy browned edges, irresistible creamy center, and peppery flavor, this mac and cheese wins on all counts.

ACTIVE 30 MIN; TOTAL 1 HR 30 MIN; SERVES 8

1 lb. dried spaghetti

1½ cups milk

3 oz. Parmigiano-Reggiano cheese, grated (about ¾ cup)

3 large eggs, lightly beaten

2½ tsp. black pepper

2 tsp. kosher salt

6 oz. Fontina cheese, shredded (2 cups), divided

6 oz. sharp white cheddar cheese, shredded (2 cups), divided

Unsalted butter, for greasing

1 Preheat oven to 425°F. Bring a large pot of salted water to a boil. Add spaghetti, and cook according to package directions for al dente; drain.

2 Mix spaghetti, milk, Parmigiano, eggs, pepper, salt, and 1½ cups each of Fontina and cheddar in a bowl. Scrape into a buttered 9-inch springform pan, then sprinkle remaining ½ cup each of Fontina and cheddar on top. Bake until cheese is melted and bubbling, 35 to 40 minutes.

3 Turn on broiler. Broil pie 8 inches from the heat until browned on top, 2 to 3 minutes. Transfer pie to a wire rack, and let cool for 15 minutes. Remove ring, cut pie into wedges, and serve. —*Justin Chapple*

WINE Pair with a silky, concentrated Italian red.

PENNE WITH TRIPLE TOMATO SAUCE

Tomato lovers will worship this rich pasta from former *F&W* senior associate recipe developer Melissa Rubel Jacobson. Using a triple hit of tomatoes (fresh, sun-dried, and tomato paste) makes this dish deeply flavorful and tomato-ey.

TOTAL 20 MIN; SERVES 4

1 lb. dried penne

2 medium tomatoes (5 oz. each), cut into 1-inch dice

4 oil-packed sun-dried tomatoes, drained

2 Tbsp. tomato paste

4 large basil leaves

1 garlic clove

⅓ cup extra-virgin olive oil

Kosher salt

Freshly ground black pepper

1 Bring a large pot of salted water to a boil; add penne, and cook until al dente.

2 Meanwhile, combine diced tomatoes, sun-dried tomatoes, tomato paste, basil, garlic, and oil in a blender; puree until smooth. Pour tomato sauce into a large bowl, and season with salt and pepper.

3 Drain pasta, add it to the sauce, and toss well to coat. Serve pasta piping hot.
—Melissa Rubel Jacobson

SPICY PEANUT NOODLES

We love Chinese peanut noodles, and this version by chef Joanne Chang stands out because of its accessibility and ease–and the fact that it's just so tasty. "My mother used to make this," Chang says. "I learned to re-create it in college, far away from any Chinese markets." Pantry staples like spaghetti and peanut butter are perfect stand-ins for the traditional ingredients. To give spaghetti the soft texture of Chinese noodles, cook it a few minutes longer than the box advises.

TOTAL 20 MIN; SERVES 6

1 lb. dried spaghetti
¾ cup smooth peanut butter
½ cup unseasoned rice vinegar, divided
3 Tbsp. plus 1 tsp. sugar
6 Tbsp. soy sauce
¼ cup water
1 Tbsp. toasted sesame oil
2 tsp. crushed red pepper
1 (2-inch) piece of fresh ginger, peeled and coarsely chopped
1 large garlic clove
3 celery ribs, thinly sliced
½ cup coarsely chopped fresh cilantro leaves and tender stems
Lime wedges, for serving

1 Cook spaghetti in a pot of boiling salted water according to package directions for al dente. Drain and rinse under cold water until cooled. Drain well.

2 Combine peanut butter, 6 tablespoons vinegar, 3 tablespoons sugar, soy sauce, water, sesame oil, red pepper, ginger, and garlic in a blender and puree. Transfer ½ cup peanut dressing to a bowl, and toss with noodles.

3 Toss celery, cilantro, remaining 2 tablespoons vinegar, and 1 teaspoon sugar in another bowl.

4 Transfer noodles to bowls, and drizzle with remaining peanut dressing. Top with celery, and serve with lime wedges. —*Joanne Chang*

MAKE AHEAD The peanut dressing can be refrigerated for 2 days.

JOANNE CHANG

You may know Joanne Chang for her incredible sticky buns or her delicious, peanutty dan dan noodles, but the star chef's path to success in the restaurant industry was roundabout: Chang, who studied math and economics as an undergrad at Harvard, started out in finance.

At 24, she was working as a management consultant at The Monitor Group in Cambridge when she was tasked with interviewing prospective hires. One of her questions to them—"If you won the lottery today, what would you do? Where would you go?"—inspired self-reflection on her own part; while listening to people's answers, it dawned on Chang that her own dream job wasn't the one she was doing. Instead, she realized, she wanted to pursue her lifelong love of baking in a professional setting. (As a college student, she had often sold chocolate chip cookies to her fellow classmates to earn extra cash.) Without any formal training, Chang decided to set off on a career in food and took a job as a *garde-manger* at Biba in Boston.

After working as the pastry chef at Rialto and in the cake department of New York's Payard Patisserie, Chang opened Flour Bakery + Café in Boston. While expanding Flour (there are now four outposts), she also collaborated with her husband on their eponymous restaurant, Myers + Chang, which serves Asian dishes inspired by the classic Chinese and Taiwanese food Chang ate during childhood.

In 2016, Chang was named Outstanding Baker by the James Beard Foundation. And although she doesn't do hands-on baking on a day-to-day basis anymore, her passion for pastry hasn't flagged.

"People ask me all the time if I miss baking. As a pastry chef, I spent the first part of my career in a baggy, oversized polyester chef's coat working in windowless basements for 10 to 12 hours a day, baking cakes, mixing doughs, shaping breads, lining and filling tarts. I loved it! I reveled in the minutia of making every pastry perfect and tasting every sauce and cookie and cake (nope, it never gets old)," she says. "So do I miss baking? You bet I do. But do I love my current gig of managing teams, training my managers to be great leaders . . . and still tasting every sauce, cookie, and cake scrap I can get my hands on? You bet I do."

SPAGHETTI WITH CLAMS AND BRAISED GREENS

We didn't think spaghetti and clams could get better than the garlicky classic until chef Ashley Christensen of Poole's Diner in Raleigh, North Carolina, created a version that forever changed the way we look at this dish. Her method is to steam the clams in wine, then puree the resulting broth with roasted red peppers, creating a briny, rich, deeply flavorful sauce that clings to the pasta—no leaving any delicious sauce behind in the bowl. Adding a hefty load of Swiss chard helps to amp up the flavor, creating a fabulously satisfying one-dish wonder.

TOTAL 45 MIN; SERVES 4

½ cup extra-virgin olive oil, divided

8 garlic cloves, crushed, divided

48 littleneck clams, scrubbed

2 cups dry white wine

2 jarred roasted red peppers, drained

1 tsp. crushed red pepper

1 lb. Swiss chard or collard greens, stemmed and chopped (about 8 cups)

Kosher salt

Freshly ground black pepper

½ lb. dried spaghetti

2 oz. Parmigiano-Reggiano cheese, grated (about ½ cup), plus more for serving

2 Tbsp. cold unsalted butter, cubed

1 tsp. lemon zest plus 1 Tbsp. fresh lemon juice

1 Heat ¼ cup oil in a large pot over medium. Add 4 cloves garlic, and cook, stirring occasionally, 1 minute. Stir in clams; add wine, and bring to a boil over medium-high. Cover and cook, stirring occasionally, until clams open, 5 to 7 minutes. As clams open, transfer them to a baking sheet. Discard any clams that do not open. Pour cooking liquid through a wire-mesh strainer into a blender. Add roasted red peppers; puree until smooth.

2 Wash out pot. Add remaining ¼ cup oil, and heat over medium. Add remaining 4 cloves garlic, and cook, stirring, 1 minute. Stir in red pepper. Working in batches, add Swiss chard, cooking until wilted before adding more, about 3 minutes per batch. Stir in roasted pepper mixture; season with salt and black pepper.

3 Cook spaghetti in a large pot of boiling salted water according to package directions for al dente; drain. Add pasta, cheese, butter, and zest and juice to chard mixture. Add clams; toss until heated through. Divide pasta mixture among shallow serving bowls; garnish with cheese. —*Ashley Christensen*

WINE Pair with a lemon-limey, lightly tingly Vinho Verde.

Desserts

DEEP-DISH ALL-AMERICAN CINNAMON APPLE PIE

Of the dozens of apple pie recipes we published in 40 years, this is hands down the best. It comes as no surprise that it's the creative genius of pastry queen Rose Levy Beranbaum. Interestingly, this pie was developed to be "slimmer, trimmer, but just as tasty" as its double-crusted counterpart. "Bigger is not necessarily better, and neither is sweeter," said Beranbaum. Not convinced? Try a slice. You'll see.

ACTIVE 30 MIN; TOTAL 2 HR 40 MIN; SERVES 8

PÂTE BRISÉE PIE SHELL

- 1⅓ cups all-purpose flour (about 5¾ oz.), plus more for work surface
- ½ cup unsalted butter (4 oz.), chilled and cut into ½-inch pieces
- ½ tsp. fine sea salt
- 3 to 5 Tbsp. ice water

APPLE PIE

- Pâte Brisée Pie Shell
- ⅓ cup apricot preserves, melted and strained, divided
- 3 lb. Rhode Island Greening or Granny Smith apples, peeled, quartered, and cut into ¼-inch-thick slices
- ¼ cup packed light brown sugar
- ¼ cup granulated sugar
- 1½ tsp. ground cinnamon
- ¼ tsp. grated fresh nutmeg
- ¼ tsp. fine sea salt
- 2 Tbsp. unsalted butter (1 oz.)
- 4 tsp. cornstarch

1 MAKE THE PÂTE BRISÉE PIE SHELL Combine flour, butter, and salt in a food processor. Pulse until mixture resembles small peas. Sprinkle 3 tablespoons ice water over flour mixture; process 3 seconds. Toss lightly with a fork to mix in any dry particles of flour. If dough does not hold together when pinched, add up to 2 tablespoons water, 1 tablespoon at a time, pulsing 3 times between additions. (Do not overmix.)

2 Turn dough out onto a lightly floured surface, and knead lightly just until it holds together. Shape into a ball. Wrap loosely in plastic wrap, and flatten into a 6-inch disk. Chill 1 hour or up to overnight.

3 Let dough stand at room temperature until malleable, about 10 minutes. Unwrap dough; roll into a 16-inch circle on a lightly floured surface. Fit dough into a 9-inch springform pan. Press pastry on bottom and up sides of pan; trim off any excess dough. Cover with plastic wrap. Chill 1 hour, then freeze 15 minutes.

4 Preheat oven to 425°F. Line chilled pie shell with parchment paper; fill with pie weights or dried beans, making sure to push them up well against sides. Bake in preheated oven until pie shell is almost dry, 20 to 25 minutes. Remove parchment paper and weights; prick bottom and sides all over with a fork. Bake until golden brown, 5 to 8 minutes. Turn off oven, leave oven door slightly ajar, and let pie shell stand in hot oven 15 minutes. Transfer pie shell in pan to a wire rack to cool completely, about 30 minutes.

5 MAKE THE APPLE PIE Brush inside of baked pie shell with 2 tablespoons apricot preserves. Place apples, brown sugar, granulated sugar, cinnamon, nutmeg, and salt in a large bowl; toss to combine. Let stand until apples release about ½ cup liquid, 30 minutes to 1 hour. Drain apple liquid into a small, heavy saucepan. Set apples aside. Add butter to pan; bring to a boil over medium-high; cook, stirring occasionally, until liquid is reduced to about ⅓ cup, 3 to 5 minutes.

6 Preheat oven to 425°F. Toss apples with cornstarch. Arrange half the apples on bottom of pie shell; drizzle with half the reduced apple syrup. Arrange remaining apples in overlapping concentric circles on top, starting from outside and working in; drizzle with remaining apple syrup. (The apples will be heaped above the top of pie shell but will sink during baking.)

7 Cut a round of aluminum foil to fit over top of pie; pull edges of foil up and crimp to create a small dome. Tent pie with foil, and bake in preheated oven until apples are tender when pierced with a paring knife, 1 hour to 1 hour and 15 minutes. Remove foil; bake until tops of apples are lightly browned, 5 to 8 minutes.

8 Warm remaining apricot preserves, and brush over top of hot pie. Cool pie in pan on a wire rack 30 minutes. Transfer pie from pan to a serving platter. Serve warm, or at room temperature. — *Rose Levy Berenbaum*

PLUM GALETTE

We all learned an invaluable trick with this perfect fruit tart from Jaques Pépin. He mixes a little sugar with ground almonds and flour and spreads it over the pastry before adding the fruit. This soaks up the extra juices and creates the most sublime, crisp crust. The trick works for all galettes with juicy fruit fillings.

ACTIVE 30 MIN; TOTAL 2 HR; SERVES 8

PATE BRISEE

- 1½ cups all-purpose flour, (about 6⅜ oz.)
- ¾ cup unsalted butter (6 oz.), cut into ½-inch pieces
- ¼ tsp. kosher salt
- ⅓ cup ice water

FILLING

- ¼ cup plus ⅓ cup sugar, divided
- 3 Tbsp. ground almonds
- 3 Tbsp. all-purpose flour
- 2½ lb. large plums, halved, pitted, and cut into ½-inch wedges
- 3 Tbsp. unsalted butter (about 1½ oz.), cut into small bits
- ½ cup good-quality plum, apricot, or raspberry preserves, strained if chunky or seedy

1 MAKE THE PÂTE BRISÉE Combine flour, butter, and salt in a food processor. Process for 5 seconds; the butter should still be in pieces. Add ice water, and process just until dough comes together, for 5 seconds longer. (Butter should still be visible.)

2 Remove dough from processor and gather it into a ball. On a lightly floured surface, roll out dough into a 16- x 18-inch oval, 1/16 to ⅛ inch thick. Drape dough over rolling pin and transfer to a large, heavy baking sheet. Chill dough until firm, about 20 minutes. Preheat oven to 400°F.

3 MAKE THE FILLING Combine ¼ cup sugar, almonds, and flour in a small bowl. Spread mixture evenly over dough to within 2 inches of the edge. Arrange plum wedges on top and dot with butter. Sprinkle all but 1 teaspoon of the remaining ⅓ cup sugar over fruit. Fold edge of dough up over plums to create a 2-inch border. (If dough feels cold and firm, wait for a few minutes until it softens to prevent it from cracking.) Sprinkle border with reserved 1 teaspoon sugar.

4 Bake galette in middle of oven for about 1 hour, until fruit is very soft and crust is richly browned. If any juices have leaked onto baking sheet, slide a knife under galette to release it. Evenly brush preserves over hot fruit; brush some up onto crust, too, if desired. Transfer pie to a wire rack, and let cool to room temperature before serving. – *Jaques Pépin*

JACQUES PÉPIN

Former *F&W* Executive Editor Tina Ujaki has referred to Jacques Pépin as a "food whisperer." She described an experience she had with him as a case in point. "I would meet him at the French Culinary Institute (now called the International Culinary Center) in New York City, where he is now a dean, to plan stories. We would have lunch (three courses with wine, always) at the school's restaurant, then go back into the kitchens to meet the students. One day, the lesson was roast chicken. As we walked past the ovens, Jacques pointed out which birds were done and which needed more time—without looking. How did he know? By listening to the fat splattering in the pans."

Pépin grew up in the kitchen. His mother was a chef and his parents owned a restaurant, Le Pelican, in his hometown near Lyon, France. At age 13, he quit school to apprentice in a kitchen. At 17, he moved to Paris and worked in the kitchens of Plaza Athénée, Maxim's, and Fouquet's. After a stint as a chef for the French Navy, he became the personal chef to three French heads of state—including Charles de Gaulle, from 1956 to 1958. In 1959, he came to the United States. Although he planned to stay just a few years, he loved it here and made a life—and a tremendous impact—on so many young American chefs.

In 2017, in honor of his 80th birthday and final PBS series, we asked a few of his biggest fans to tell us how this extraordinary teacher changed the way they cook, think, and live.

Thomas Keller had this to say: "What separates a good chef from a great chef? I once asked Jacques Pépin.

"He said: 'To be a good chef you have to be a good technician. To be a great chef you have to be a good technician, but you also have to have talent, and you have to have love.' Jacques has always reminded us that one cannot cook indifferently. He also has taught us that food doesn't make sense unless you share it with someone. This is the essence of Jacques: giving invaluable culinary and life lessons. It is my belief that the best chefs are the ones who came before us, the innovators and influencers whose experience and expertise paved the way for us. Jacques Pépin has helped elevate cooking from a mere job to a respected field pursued by professionals."

BERRY VINEGAR TART

In this clever riff on lemon pie, former *F&W* Food Editor Laura Rege fills a crunchy graham cracker crust with a sweet and tangy curd made with blackberry vinegar, fresh raspberries, and a hint of virgin coconut oil. It's ideal for anyone who enjoys a dessert with some pucker.

ACTIVE 30 MIN; TOTAL 3 HR; SERVES 8

- 12 whole graham crackers
- 1¼ cups plus 1 Tbsp. granulated sugar, divided
- ¾ tsp. kosher salt, divided
- 5 Tbsp. unsalted butter, melted
- 8 large egg yolks
- ½ cup blackberry vinegar
- 2 Tbsp. cornstarch
- 6 oz. raspberries (1¾ cups), plus more for garnish
- 1 Tbsp. virgin coconut oil
- ¾ cup heavy cream

1 Preheat oven to 350°F. Combine the graham crackers, ¼ cup sugar, and ¼ teaspoon salt in a food processor, and pulse until fine crumbs form. Add the butter and pulse until incorporated. Press the crumbs evenly on the bottom and up the sides of a 13- x 4-inch fluted tart pan with a removable bottom. Bake the crust until fragrant and browned, about 12 minutes. Transfer to a wire rack, and let cool completely.

2 Whisk egg yolks and 1 cup sugar in a medium saucepan until blended. Whisk in vinegar, cornstarch, and remaining ½ teaspoon salt, and cook over medium, continuously whisking until bubbling, about 5 minutes. Add raspberries and return to a simmer. Whisk until berries are broken down and filling is very thick, about 5 minutes longer.

3 Remove saucepan from heat, and whisk in coconut oil. Pour filling through a fine wire-mesh strainer into a medium bowl, pressing on the solids. (There should be just over 1 cup of custard.) Pour custard into crust, cover with plastic wrap, and refrigerate until cold, at least 2 hours.

4 Transfer tart to a platter. Whisk cream with remaining 1 tablespoon sugar in a large bowl until medium peaks form. Dollop whipped cream on top of tart, garnish with raspberries, and serve. — *Laura Rege*

MOM'S CITRUS MERINGUE PIE

Legendary culinary historian, teacher, and author Jessica B. Harris has spent years documenting the foodways of the African diaspora. Harris contributed several articles to *F&W* in the 1980s and 1990s, including a piece on her Southern family's traditions and heirloom recipes, inspired by her mother and two grandmothers. Of the three women, Harris said, "Each was representative of the major African-American culinary traditions that have marked America." Her mother's influence included a spectacular citrus meringue pie that uses fresh lemon and lime juices baked in a pastry shell made with fresh orange juice.

ACTIVE 35 MIN; TOTAL 6 HR 25 MIN; SERVES 8

PREBAKED ORANGE PASTRY SHELL

- 1½ cups all-purpose flour (about 6⅜ oz.), plus more for dusting
- ½ tsp. fine sea salt
- ⅓ cup chilled lard or 7 Tbsp. vegetable shortening
- 5 to 7 Tbsp. chilled fresh orange juice (from 2 oranges)

PIE

- ½ cup cornstarch (about 2¼ oz.)
- 2½ tsp. lemon zest plus 6 Tbsp. fresh lemon juice (from 3 lemons), divided
- ¼ cup fresh lime juice (from 2 limes)
- 3 cups water
- 2½ cups granulated sugar, divided
- 2 Tbsp. unsalted butter (1 oz.), softened
- ¼ tsp. fine sea salt, divided
- 4 large eggs, separated
  Prebaked Orange Pastry Shell
- ¼ tsp. cream of tartar

1 MAKE THE PREBAKED ORANGE PASTRY SHELL Stir together flour and salt in a medium bowl. Using a pastry blender, or 2 knives, cut in lard until mixture resembles small peas. Using a fork, gradually stir in 5 tablespoons orange juice; stir until dough comes together. (Add remaining 2 tablespoons orange juice, 1 tablespoon at a time, if needed.) Shape dough into a disk. Wrap disk in plastic wrap, and chill 1 hour or up to 2 days before using.

2 Preheat oven to 350°F. Unwrap chilled dough disk, and place on a lightly floured work surface. Roll into a 12-inch circle. Without stretching dough, transfer to a 9-inch pie plate. Fold edge of dough under, and crimp edges or press with the tines of a fork. Using a fork, prick bottom of dough all over. Freeze 15 minutes. Bake until golden brown, about 30 minutes. Transfer to a wire rack, and let cool completely before filling, about 30 minutes.

3 MAKE THE PIE Preheat oven to 350°F. Stir together cornstarch, lemon juice, and lime juice in a medium nonreactive saucepan until cornstarch dissolves. Stir in 3 cups water, 2 cups sugar, butter, ⅛ teaspoon salt, and lemon zest. Bring to a boil over medium-low, stirring constantly with a wooden spoon, about 15 minutes. (Mixture will thicken as it cooks.) Remove from heat.

4 Whisk egg yolks in a large bowl. Gradually whisk in hot lemon-lime mixture. Press a piece of plastic wrap directly onto surface, and let cool 30 minutes. Pour filling into prebaked orange pastry shell. Set aside.

5 Beat egg whites and remaining ⅛ teaspoon salt with a stand mixer fitted with the whisk attachment on medium speed until frothy, about 1 minute. Gradually add cream of tartar and remaining ½ cup sugar, beating well. Continue beating until mixture forms stiff, glossy peaks, about 4 minutes.

6 Gently dollop meringue over lemon-lime filling. Using the back of a spoon, spread meringue to edges. Swirl decoratively with spoon. Bake until meringue is golden brown, about 20 minutes. Transfer to a wire rack, and let cool to room temperature, about 2 hours. Transfer to refrigerator until well chilled, about 3 hours.
—*Jessica B. Harris*

NOTE Because there is lard in the dough, this pastry gets very soft as it comes to room temperature, so roll it out as quickly as possible.

RASPBERRY WHOLE WHEAT BUTTER CAKE

This raspberry cake from pastry gurus Zoe Nathan and Laurel Almerinda of Huckleberry Cafe in Santa Monica is made with a combination of almond flour, whole wheat flour, all-purpose flour, and wheat germ. Despite its nut-flour and whole-grain base, it's buttery and tender–and the rich, nutty flavor is a beautiful thing paired with the tart, acidic berries.

ACTIVE 30 MIN; TOTAL 2 HR 40 MIN; MAKES ONE 10-INCH CAKE

- 1 cup unsalted butter (8 oz.), plus more for greasing, softened
- 1¼ cups almond flour (about 4¼ oz.)
- ¾ cup whole wheat flour (about 3 oz.)
- ½ cup all-purpose flour (about 2⅛ oz.)
- ¼ cup wheat germ
- 2¼ tsp. baking powder
- 2 cups plus 2 Tbsp. granulated sugar, divided
- 2¼ tsp. kosher salt
- 2 tablespoons pure vanilla extract
- 7 large eggs
- 2 cups fresh raspberries, plus more for serving
- Whipped cream, for serving

1 Preheat oven to 350°F. Butter a 10-inch round cake pan, and line bottom with parchment paper; butter parchment paper.

2 Whisk together almond flour, whole wheat flour, all-purpose flour, wheat germ, and baking powder in a medium bowl until well blended. Set aside. Beat butter, 2 cups sugar, and salt with a stand mixer fitted with a paddle attachment, or using a handheld electric mixer, on medium speed until pale yellow and fluffy, about 3 minutes. Add vanilla, then beat in eggs 1 at a time, scraping down sides and bottom of bowl (the mixture will look broken). Add flour mixture, and beat on low speed just until incorporated and batter is smooth. Scrape batter into prepared pan, and smooth top. Arrange 2 cups of raspberries in a single layer on top, then sprinkle with remaining 2 tablespoons of sugar. Bake in preheated oven until cake is golden and a wooden pick inserted in center comes out clean, about 50 minutes. Transfer to a rack to cool for 15 minutes.

3 Run a thin, sharp knife around edge of cake. Invert cake onto a large plate; peel off parchment paper. Turn cake right side up on a serving plate, and let cool until warm, about 1 hour. Serve with whipped cream and raspberries. —*Zoe Nathan and Laurel Almerinda*

MAKE AHEAD The cake can be stored at room temperature overnight.

ULTIMATE CHOCOLATE MOUSSE

To celebrate chocolate in its most delectable guises, we asked some of the best cooks–Julia Child, James Beard, Maida Heatter, and more–to share their favorite chocolate recipes. Craig Claiborne, who was the *New York Times* restaurant critic and one of the top food journalists at the time, shared his remarkable chocolate mousse, which could reliably be whipped up without tremendous effort. In his original piece on the recipe, Claiborne wrote, "Once in a rare while, I discover a formula for a dish that seems the ultimate, the definitive, the *ne plus ultra*. I am convinced that the finest chocolate mousse creation ever whipped up in my kitchen is the one printed here. As if you didn't know, mousse means 'foam' in French. This mousse is the foamiest." The key to this recipe is to use the very best semisweet dark chocolate you can find–we like Valrhona. The better the chocolate, the better the mousse.

ACTIVE 30 MIN; TOTAL 4 HR 30 MIN; SERVES 12

- 8 oz. semisweet dark chocolate, broken into ½-inch pieces
- 6 large eggs, separated
- 3 Tbsp. water
- ¼ cup (2 oz.) sweet liqueur (such as Chartreuse, amaretto, mandarin, or Grand Marnier)
- 2 cups heavy cream
- 6 Tbsp. granulated sugar, divided

  Whipped cream and grated chocolate, for garnish

1 Place chocolate in top of a double boiler over simmering water, and cook over low, stirring occasionally, until chocolate is melted. Remove from heat, and set aside.

2 Place egg yolks and 3 tablespoons water in a heavy saucepan; cook over very low, whisking vigorously and constantly, until yolks begin to foam and thicken, about 6 minutes. Whisk in liqueur, and cook, whisking constantly, until sauce thickens enough to coat the back of a spoon, 6 to 8 minutes. (The sauce should achieve the consistency of a hollandaise or sabayon.) Remove from heat. Pour through a fine wire-mesh strainer into a bowl; discard solids.

3 Fold melted chocolate into sauce. Transfer chocolate mixture to a large bowl, and set aside.

4 Beat cream with an electric mixer on high-speed until stiff peaks form, about 2 minutes, beating in 2 tablespoons sugar toward the end. Fold into chocolate mixture.

5 Beat egg whites with an electric mixer fitted with the whisk attachment on high speed until soft peaks form, about 1 minute. Beat in remaining ¼ cup sugar, and continue beating until stiff peaks form, about 2 minutes. Fold into chocolate-cream mixture.

6 Spoon mousse into a bowl, and chill 4 hours or up to 24 hours until ready to serve. Garnish servings with whipped cream and grated chocolate. —*Craig Claiborne*

MOM'S CHOCOLATE CAKE

Longtime *F&W* Test Kitchen Supervisor Marcia Kiesel was credited for this very moist, very chocolaty, easy-to-make layer cake, but the recipe originated with a waitress at the Beekman Arms in Rhinebeck, New York, who got it from her mother. The secret is unsweetened chocolate in the batter, which lends the cake a rich, deep chocolate flavor. The thick, creamy frosting hits just the right balance, but Kiesel says, "The original was served right out of the pan, no frosting at all, and that's my favorite way to eat it."

ACTIVE 35 MIN; TOTAL 1 HR 55 MIN; SERVES 10

CAKE

- 6 Tbsp. unsalted butter (3 oz.), plus more for greasing
- 2 cups all-purpose flour (about 8½ oz.), plus more for dusting
- 2 tsp. baking powder
- 2 tsp. baking soda
- 1 tsp. fine sea salt
- 2 cups granulated sugar
- 2 cups water
- 4 oz. unsweetened baking chocolate, roughly chopped (about ¾ cup)
- 1 tsp. pure vanilla extract
- 2 large eggs, lightly beaten

CHOCOLATE FROSTING

- 1½ cups granulated sugar
- 1⅓ cups heavy cream
- 6 oz. unsweetened baking chocolate, roughly chopped
- ½ cup plus 2 Tbsp. unsalted butter
- 1½ tsp. pure vanilla extract
- ⅛ tsp. fine sea salt

1 MAKE THE CAKE Preheat oven to 350°F. Butter and flour two 8-inch round cake pans. Line bottoms with rounds of parchment paper. Sift together flour, baking powder, baking soda, and salt in a medium bowl; set aside.

2 Stir together sugar and 2 cups water in a medium saucepan. Bring to a boil over high, and cook, stirring, until sugar dissolves, about 2 minutes. Transfer mixture to bowl of a stand mixer. Add chocolate and butter, and let stand, stirring occasionally, until melted and cooled to 150°F, about 15 minutes. Stir in vanilla.

3 Add eggs to chocolate mixture; beat on medium speed until combined, about 10 seconds. Add flour mixture; beat on medium speed until smooth, stopping to scrape down sides of bowl as needed, about 2 minutes. Divide batter between prepared pans. Bake in preheated oven until tops of cakes spring back when lightly pressed, and wooden picks inserted in centers come out clean, 24 to 26 minutes. Cool cakes in pans on a wire rack 25 minutes. Invert cakes onto rack to cool completely, about 1 hour. Discard parchment.

4 MAKE THE CHOCOLATE FROSTING Stir together sugar and cream in a medium saucepan. Bring to a boil over medium-high, stirring occasionally. Reduce heat to low, and simmer until liquid reduces slightly, about 6 minutes. Pour mixture into a medium bowl, and add chocolate, butter, vanilla, and salt. Let stand, stirring occasionally, until melted, about 10 minutes.

5 Set bowl with frosting inside a larger bowl of ice water. Beat frosting with an electric mixer on medium speed until thick and glossy, stopping to scrape down sides, about 6 minutes. Remove bowl from ice water; immediately proceed to Step 6.

6 Place 1 cake on a serving plate. Using an offset metal spatula, spread one-third of frosting over top and sides of cake. Top with second cake, and frost top and sides with remaining frosting. —*Marcia Kiesel*

BITTERSWEET CHOCOLATE TART

The exquisite and rich tart of the late French chef Joel Robouchon floored us because it couldn't be perfected: With its satiny dark sheen and wonderful play of chocolate against the delicate sweet pastry, it is precisely what it needs to be. One little slice goes a long way.

ACTIVE 10 MIN; TOTAL 22 MIN; SERVES 8

SHORTBREAD PASTRY

- 1 plump vanilla bean, shelled
- 1 egg yolk, at room temperature
- 2 Tbsp. whole blanched almonds
- ½ cup confectioners' sugar, sifted
- ¾ cup all-purpose flour (about 3⅛ oz.), sifted
  Pinch of kosher salt
- 5 Tbsp. unsalted butter (about 2½ oz.), softened

TART

- ¾ cup heavy cream
- ⅓ cup milk
- 7 oz. imported bittersweet chocolate, grated or finely chopped
- 1 egg, lightly beaten
  Shortbread Pastry Shell
- ½ tsp. unsweetened cocoa powder, preferably Dutch process, for garnish (optional)

1 MAKE THE SHORTBREAD PASTRY Flatten vanilla bean and cut in half lengthwise. With a small spoon, scrape seeds into a small bowl. Add egg yolk, and stir to blend. Set aside.

2 Preheat oven to 375°F with oven rack in middle of oven. Combine almonds and sugar in a food processor, and process until finely ground. Add flour and salt, and process to blend. Add butter, and process just until mixture resembles coarse crumbs. Add egg yolk and vanilla seeds, and pulse until dough just begins to hold together, about 10 times. Do not overprocess; dough should not form a ball.

3 Transfer dough to a sheet of waxed paper. With your hands, gently form dough into a ball, handling as little as possible, and flatten into a disk. Wrap and refrigerate until well chilled, at least 1 hour or overnight.

4 Butter bottom and sides of a 9-inch fluted tart pan with removable bottom. On a lightly floured surface, roll out dough into an 11-inch circle. Transfer dough to prepared tart pan. Using your fingertips, gently press dough against fluted sides of pan. Allow about ½-inch overhang around rim of pan. Generously prick bottom of dough all over with a fork. Refrigerate until well chilled, at least 1 hour, or wrap loosely in foil and refrigerate up to 24 hours.

5 Bake in preheated oven until pastry just begins to firm up, about 5 minutes. Remove from oven, and, with a sharp knife, carefully cut off and discard overhanging pastry to make a smooth, even rim. Return shell to oven, and bake for about 15 minutes longer until pastry is well browned all over. Transfer to a wire rack to cool before filling.

6 MAKE THE TART Combine cream and milk in a medium saucepan, and bring to simmer over medium. Remove from heat, add chocolate, and stir until thoroughly melted, about 1 minute. Set aside, and let cool to lukewarm. When cooled, whisk in egg until thoroughly blended.

7 Pour filling into baked pastry shell. Bake in the middle of oven until filling is almost firm but still trembling in the center, 12 to 15 minutes. Transfer to a wire rack to cool. If desired, dust with unsweetened cocoa powder. Serve warm or at room temperature. —*Joel Robouchon*

MOLTEN CHOCOLATE CAKES

In the 1990s, molten chocolate cakes had everyone swooning. World-famous chef and restaurateur Jean-George Vongerichten is the OG of molten chocolate cakes–these are the ones that started it all. Molten chocolate cakes became famous for a reason: They're cakey on the outside with an irresistible center of warm dark chocolate flowing through the middle. The first time you try one, it may seem like magic, but this recipe is actually quite easy to make and ready in under an hour.

ACTIVE 20 MIN; TOTAL 35 MIN; SERVES 4

½ cup unsalted butter (4 oz.)

6 oz. bittersweet chocolate, preferably Valrhona

2 eggs

2 egg yolks

¼ cup granulated sugar

Pinch of kosher salt

2 Tbsp. all-purpose flour

1 Preheat oven to 450°F. Butter and lightly flour four 6-ounce ramekins. Tap out excess flour. Set ramekins on a baking sheet.

2 Melt butter with chocolate in a double boiler over shimmering water. Combine eggs, egg yolks, sugar, and salt in a medium bowl; beat until thickened and pale.

3 Whisk chocolate until smooth. Quickly fold it into egg mixture along with flour. Spoon batter into prepared ramekins, and bake until sides of cakes are firm but centers are soft, 12 minutes. Let cakes cool in ramekins for 1 minute; cover each with an inverted dessert plate. Carefully turn each one over, let stand for 10 seconds, and then unmold. Serve immediately. —*Jean-George Vongerichten*

MAKE AHEAD The batter can be refrigerated for several hours; bring to room temperature before baking.

WINE Pair with a Ruby Porto.

JEAN-GEORGES VONGERICHTEN

When Jean-Georges Vongerichten was growing up in Alsace, France, his mother and grandmother made lunch every day for the nearly 50 employees of their family-owned coal business. It was this continuous immersion in food—and a 16th birthday dinner at the 3-star Michelin-rated Auberge de l'Ill—that cemented his career choice.

He began training in a work-study program there as a teenager and went on to work with the top chefs in France into his late 20s. He helped open 10 restaurants around the world, including the Oriental Hotel in Bangkok, the Meridien Hotel in Singapore, and the Mandarin Hotel in Hong Kong. In 1985, he moved to Boston and shortly thereafter to New York, where his fresh interpretations of classic French cuisine at Lafayette in the Drake Swissôtel earned him four stars from the *New York Times* at the age of 29.

Today, he runs an empire of nearly 40 restaurants around the world, including his first restaurant, JoJo, which he opened in 1991, and the Michelin-rated flagship, Jean-Georges, opened in 1997.

No matter how wildly different the cooking appears at each of his ventures, underlying his culinary genius are a few essentials. They include an enduring love of Asian ingredients, prepared with classical technique: Lightness, which comes from vegetable juices, flavored oils, vinaigrettes, and quick broths. ("I don't want the taste of boiled stock in a sauce," he once told us.) A contrast of textures and temperatures. ("If there's no contrast, we don't do it.") And a balance of heat, tang, vibrancy of fresh herbs, and (optional) sweetness in every dish.

CHOCOLATE BROWNIE COOKIES

There is simply no improving on these cookies, which are fudgy and rich while simultaneously crispy and crackly–like crispy-chewy brownies in cookie form. Belinda Leong of b. Patisserie in San Francisco freezes the batter before baking to achieve that crackly outer layer.

ACTIVE 30 MIN; TOTAL 2 HR 30 MIN; MAKES 3 DOZEN COOKIES

1 lb. semisweet chocolate, chopped

4 Tbsp. unsalted butter (2 oz.)

4 large eggs, at room temperature

1½ cups granulated sugar

1 tsp. pure vanilla extract

¼ tsp. kosher salt

½ cup all-purpose flour, sifted (about 2⅛ oz.)

½ tsp. baking powder

1 (12-oz.) bag semisweet chocolate chips

1 Place chocolate and butter in a large bowl set over a saucepan of simmering water, and melt, stirring a few times, until smooth, about 7 minutes.

2 Beat eggs and sugar in another large bowl with an electric mixer on medium-speed until thick and pale, about 5 minutes. Beat in vanilla and salt. Using a rubber spatula, fold in the melted chocolate, then fold in flour and baking powder. Stir in chocolate chips. Scrape batter into a shallow baking dish, cover, and freeze until batter is well chilled and firm, about 1 hour.

3 Preheat oven to 350°F, and line 2 baking sheets with parchment paper. Working in batches, scoop 2-tablespoon-size mounds of dough onto prepared baking sheets, about 2 inches apart. Bake in preheated oven until cookies are dry around edges and cracked on top, 10 minutes. Let cookies cool on baking sheets for 10 minutes, then transfer to a rack to cool completely before serving. —*Belinda Leong*

BRETON BUTTER CAKE

We got our first taste of *kouign-amann*, the irresistibly sweet and flaky pastry from Brittany in Northwestern France, in 2004 from authors Naomi Duguid and Jeffrey Alford, who traveled the world in pursuit of recipes. Making *kouign-amann* is not too different from making croissants, wherein butter is folded into a rich, yeasty dough, but here it melts and browns as it bakes, producing an aroma that's both dreamy and homey. *Kouign-amann* also includes sugar, which creates crisp, golden caramelized bits that are truly impossible to resist. Duguid and Alford's brilliant version is prepared with store-bought bread or pizza dough.

ACTIVE 30 MIN; TOTAL 3 HR 30 MIN; SERVES 8

¾ cup cold salted butter (6 oz.)

1 lb. frozen white bread dough, thawed

All-purpose flour, for work surface

10 Tbsp. granulated sugar, divided

½ Tbsp. salted butter, plus more for greasing, melted

1 Place butter between 2 sheets of parchment paper; pound with a rolling pin to form a 6-inch square. Transfer butter square with parchment paper to refrigerator to chill.

2 Roll dough into a 12- x 8-inch rectangle on a lightly floured surface. Unwrap chilled butter square, and discard parchment. Place butter square on half of dough rectangle. Sprinkle butter square with 3 tablespoons sugar.

3 Fold other half of dough rectangle over butter to opposite side, and press to seal edges. Roll filled dough into a 20- x 8-inch rectangle on a lightly floured surface. Fold short ends of dough up and over to meet in middle of rectangle; brush off any excess flour. Fold dough rectangle (about 10×8 inches) in half, short end to short end, creating 4 stacked layers. Wrap in plastic wrap, and chill 20 minutes.

4 Unwrap stacked dough, and roll into a 20- x 8-inch rectangle on a lightly floured surface. Sprinkle with 3 tablespoons sugar, and repeat folding process in step 3. Wrap dough in plastic wrap, and chill 20 minutes. Repeat rolling and folding dough process a third time with 3 tablespoons sugar. Wrap in plastic wrap, and chill 20 minutes.

5 Butter a 9-inch cast-iron skillet. Roll dough into a 9-inch circle on a lightly floured surface. Place in prepared skillet, and cover loosely with plastic wrap. Let stand at room temperature until slightly puffy, about 45 minutes.

6 Preheat oven to 425°F. Brush dough with melted butter, and sprinkle with remaining 1 tablespoon sugar. Bake in preheated oven until top is golden brown and a wooden pick inserted in center comes out clean, 40 to 44 minutes, tenting with aluminum foil after 20 minutes if necessary to prevent excessive browning. Carefully transfer hot cake to a serving platter. Let cool 30 minutes. Cut into wedges, and serve. —*Naomi Duguid and Jeffrey Alford*

NOTE The cake can be kept at room temperature overnight, but it's best eaten the day it's made.

VANILLA BEAN CHEESECAKE
WITH WALNUT CRUST

Hands down, this cheesecake recipe from author Peggy Cullen is one of the most delicious cheesecakes we ever tried. It's a magical combo of the sugary and toasty walnut crust, the ethereal cheesecake filling, and the tangy sour cream topping.

ACTIVE 20 MIN; TOTAL 4 HR 45 MIN, PLUS OVERNIGHT CHILLING; SERVES 8 TO 10

1½ cups walnut pieces

1¾ cups granulated sugar, divided

4 Tbsp. unsalted butter (2 oz.), melted

2 cups sour cream

1 Tbsp. pure vanilla extract, divided

2 lb. cream cheese, softened

1 vanilla bean, split lengthwise, seeds scraped

4 large eggs, at room temperature

¼ tsp. pure almond extract

½ cup heavy cream

1 Preheat oven to 350°F. Butter a 10-inch springform pan. Combine walnuts and ¼ cup sugar in a food processor, and pulse until finely ground. Add butter; pulse until mixture resembles moist sand. Press crumbs into bottom of pan. Bake until browned around the edges, 12 minutes.

2 Mix sour cream, ¼ cup sugar, and 1 teaspoon vanilla in a small bowl.

3 Reduce oven temperature to 300°F. Beat cream cheese, remaining 1¼ cups sugar, and vanilla seeds with a stand mixer fitted with a paddle attachment, or using a handheld electric mixer, on low speed just until combined. Beat in eggs, 1 at a time, scraping down bowl between additions. Add remaining 2 teaspoons vanilla and almond extract. Slowly beat in cream until smooth. Pour cheesecake batter into pan, and bake until lightly golden and slightly jiggly in the center, for 65 to 70 minutes.

4 Immediately pour sour cream topping over cheesecake, and smooth surface. Return cheesecake to oven, and bake 5 minutes longer. Transfer to a rack, and let cool to room temperature. Run a sharp, thin-bladed knife around cake, then remove ring. Refrigerate cake for 3 hours, then cover loosely with plastic wrap and refrigerate overnight before serving. —*Peggy Cullen*

GRAND MARNIER SOUFFLÉ

In the inaugural issue of *F&W*, legendary chef Jacques Pépin shared his recipe for the perfect soufflé. "Why their awesome mystique?" we asked. "Why does the idea of making one turn fearless kitchen lions into cowering lambs?" Pépin, who had recently published his tome of French cooking, *La Technique*, was the perfect teacher to introduce readers to the method for making "towering, golden-roofed, steamily fragrant" soufflés, giving detailed directions on everything from preparing the dish with a paper collar to beating the egg whites properly. This ethereal recipe is just as good today as it was 40-plus years ago.

ACTIVE 20 MIN; TOTAL 1 HR 15 MIN; SERVES 6

SOUFFLÉ

- 3 Tbsp. granulated sugar
- 3 Tbsp. all-purpose flour
- Unsalted butter, softened, for greasing
- Crème Pâtissière (recipe follows), at room temperature
- 2 Tbsp. Grand Marnier
- 1 Tbsp. orange zest
- 6 large egg whites, at room temperature
- Powdered sugar, for garnish

1 MAKE THE SOUFFLÉ Preheat oven to 375°F with oven rack in lower third of oven. Stir together granulated sugar and flour in a small bowl; set aside. Cut a 24- x 12-inch piece of parchment paper; fold lengthwise 3 times (letter-style). Wrap paper around outside top of a 1-quart soufflé dish to form a collar extending 2 inches above rim; secure tightly with string or tape. Rub inside of soufflé dish and parchment collar with butter. Dust with sugar mixture, shaking out excess. Chill dish at least 15 minutes.

2 Stir together Crème Pâtissière, Grand Marnier, and orange zest in a large bowl. Beat egg whites with a stand mixer on medium-speed until glossy and stiff peaks form, about 4 minutes. Whisk about one-third of egg whites into Crème Pâtissière mixture until well incorporated. Gently fold in remaining egg whites until just incorporated. Pour mixture into prepared dish. Place dish on a rimmed baking sheet, and bake in preheated oven until soufflé is puffed and golden brown, 40 to 45 minutes. Sprinkle with powdered sugar. Serve immediately. —*Jacques Pépin*

CRÈME PÂTISSIÈRE Whisk together ⅔ cup granulated sugar, 3 large egg yolks, and 1 teaspoon pure vanilla extract in a medium bowl until mixture is pale yellow and "makes ribbons," 3 to 4 minutes. Add 3 tablespoons all-purpose flour; whisk until smooth. Bring 1 cup whole milk to a boil in a medium saucepan over medium, about 3 minutes. Gradually add milk to egg yolk mixture, whisking constantly. Return mixture to saucepan. Bring to a boil over medium, whisking constantly, about 3 minutes. Boil mixture, whisking constantly, 1 minute. Transfer mixture to a medium bowl; press plastic wrap directly onto surface. Let cool to room temperature, about 1 hour. Mixture can be chilled, covered, up to 3 days. —*Jacques Pépin*

STICKY RICE COCONUT BREAD

Bibingka is a traditional Filipino coconut-rice bread that's more like a cake. This version from chef Dale Talde is made with a combination of sweet rice flour, shredded coconut, and coconut milk. It makes for a sweet and sticky confection we couldn't stop eating.

ACTIVE 30 MIN; TOTAL 2 HR; MAKES ONE 10-INCH ROUND BREAD

BIBINGKA

- Banana leaves, rinsed and patted dry
- 1 lb. sweet rice flour (3½ cups)
- ½ cup unsweetened shredded coconut
- 1 tsp. baking powder
- ¼ tsp. kosher salt
- 1 stick unsalted butter, softened
- 2 cups granulated sugar
- 4 large eggs
- 1 (14-oz.) can unsweetened coconut milk
- 1 cup sour cream
- 1 tsp. pure vanilla extract
- Sweetened shredded coconut, for garnish

BUTTER

- 1 stick unsalted butter, softened
- ¼ cup maple syrup, at room temperature
- 1 tsp. black pepper
- ½ tsp. kosher salt

1 MAKE THE BIBINGKA Preheat oven to 350°F. Line a 10-inch cast-iron skillet with banana leaves. Whisk together flour, shredded coconut, baking powder, and salt in a medium bow. Beat butter, sugar, and eggs with a stand mixer fitted with a paddle attachment on medium speed until fluffy, 1 to 2 minutes. Beat in coconut milk, sour cream, and vanilla until incorporated. Add in shredded coconut and flour mixture, and beat on low speed until just incorporated. Scrape batter into prepared skillet.

2 Bake bread until edges are lightly browned and center is just set, about 1 hour. Garnish with sweetened shredded coconut, and let cool for 30 minutes.

3 MAKE THE BUTTER Meanwhile, combine butter, maple syrup, pepper, and salt in a small bowl, and blend using a fork. Serve bread with maple butter. —*Dale Talde*

NOTE Frozen banana leaves are available at large supermarkets. To bake the bread in individual portions, spoon the batter into six 1½-cup gratin dishes lined with banana leaves. Bake for 50 minutes.

WHOLE-FRUIT ROCKET POPS

Food writer, cookbook author, and *Top Chef* judge Gail Simmons pays homage to one of her favorite treats from her childhood–making it sweet enough to please children and whole-some enough to delight parents. Gail's version bursts with deep hues and summer flavor with an adult approach: layered with strawberry-lime, coconut-banana and ginger, and blueberry-mint. Making the simple base for the layers is easy using a home blender; just be sure to freeze each layer sufficiently before pouring in the next, and use a small funnel to get even layers and keep pop mold sides clean. Rest assured, the kids will come running for these delightful summer treats!

ACTIVE 35 MIN; TOTAL 6 HR, 50 MIN; SERVES 8

½ cup granulated sugar

½ cup water

1 cup fresh strawberries, stemmed

1 tsp. lime zest plus 3 Tbsp. fresh lime juice (from 2 limes), divided

⅓ cup unsweetened coconut milk, well shaken and stirred

⅓ cup sliced banana

1½ tsp. grated peeled fresh ginger

1 cup fresh blueberries

2 tsp. finely chopped fresh mint

1 Bring sugar and ½ cup water to a boil in a small saucepan over medium-high. Reduce heat to medium-low; cook, stirring occasionally, until sugar dissolves, about 3 minutes. Transfer simple syrup to a small heatproof bowl; let cool completely, about 1 hour.

2 Place strawberries, lime zest, 2 tablespoons lime juice, and 2 tablespoons simple syrup in a blender; process until smooth, about 20 seconds. Pour mixture evenly into 8 (2½-ounce) rocket pop molds (about 4 teaspoons each). Cover molds with plastic wrap; freeze until just set, 45 minutes to 1 hour.

3 Wipe blender clean. Add coconut milk, banana, ginger, and 2 tablespoons simple syrup to blender; process until smooth, about 20 seconds. Uncover pop molds. Pour mixture evenly over strawberry mixture in pop molds (about 4 teaspoons each). Recover with plastic wrap; freeze until just set, 45 minutes to 1 hour.

4 Wipe blender clean. Add blueberries, mint, 2 tablespoons simple syrup, and remaining 1 tablespoon lime juice to blender; process until smooth, about 20 seconds. (Reserve remaining simple syrup for another use.) Uncover pop molds. Pour blueberry mixture evenly over coconut mixture in pop molds (about 4 teaspoons each). Insert pop mold sticks into pops; freeze until completely frozen, about 4 hours. To serve, run molds under warm water for a few seconds, and gently pull ice pops out of molds. —*Gail Simmons*

ALMOST-INSTANT SOFT SERVE

F&W Culinary Director Justin Chapple launched his Mad Genius platform to introduce the *F&W* audience to smart, fun food hacks. This one was inspired by the Spanish chef Ferran Adrià of the late El Bulli, who made an ingenious ice cream by blending frozen fruit with sugar and fromage blanc—no ice-cream maker needed. Justin swapped in sweetened condensed milk to make the recipe even more accessible. The creamy, sherbet-style dessert is one for the ages: It uses just four ingredients and comes together with a quick whirl of the food processor. The frozen treat can be eaten like soft serve after about 3 hours or allowed to harden in the freezer for a firmer frozen treat.

ACTIVE 5 MIN; TOTAL 3 HR 15 MIN; SERVES 8

1½ lb. frozen strawberries, mango chunks, or blueberries

¾ cup sweetened condensed milk

½ tsp. vanilla extract

Pinch of kosher salt

Combine frozen fruit, sweetened condensed milk, vanilla, and a generous pinch of salt in a food processor, and pulse until fruit is finely chopped. Puree until smooth, scraping down sides as needed, 3 to 4 minutes. Serve immediately, or transfer to a metal baking pan, and cover with plastic wrap. Freeze until just firm, about 3 hours. Let stand at room temperature 10 minutes before serving. Freeze up to 3 days. —*Justin Chapple*

Grilled Greens with Popped Mustard Seeds and Ginger, page 93

INDEX

Chicken Biryani, page 162

Chicken Pho, page 43

CONTRIBUTORS

JENNIFER CAUSEY 9, 19, 22, 29, 33, 87, 92, 105, 120, 123, 138, 141, 145, 163, 166, 170, 181, 182, 185, 192, 195, 198, 202, 215, 216, 227, 241, 242, 251, 256, 260, 264

GREG DUPREE 25, 45, 46, 50, 54, 59, 66, 73, 77, 78, 81, 84, 90, 112, 118, 129, 133, 137, 142, 151, 152, 155, 156, 159, 169, 172, 175, 176, 189, 201, 204, 224, 233, 237, 238, 239, 248, 249, 252, 253, 270

BOBBY FISHER 95

ETHAN HILL 38

CHRISTOPHER HIRSCHEIMER 126, 160

CHRISTINA HOLMES 222, 247

MATTHEW HRANEK 186

JOHN KERNICK 34, 69, 108, 115

EVA KOLENKO 96, 130

JEREMY LANGE 221

JONATHAN LOVEKIN 259

DAVID MALOSH 42, 269

CON POULOS 56, 62, 83, 99, 100, 104, 146, 230, 234, 255

VICTOR PROTASIO cover, 13, 21, 41, 65, 103, 111, 207, 208, back cover

ANDREW PURCELL 212

FREDRIKA ST JARNE 119, 211

CHRISTOPHER TESTANI 27, 36, 53

ANNA WILLIAMS 70

CONVERSION CHART

BASIC MEASUREMENTS

GALLON	QUART	PINT	CUP	OUNCE	TBSP	TSP	DROPS
1 gal	4 qt	8 pt	16 c	128 fl oz			
½ gal	2 qt	4 pt	8 c	64 fl oz			
¼ gal	1 qt	2 pt	4 c	32 fl oz			
	½ qt	1 pt	2 c	16 fl oz			
	¼ qt	½ pt	1 c	8 fl oz	16 Tbsp		
			⅞ c	7 fl oz	14 Tbsp		
			¾ c	6 fl oz	12 Tbsp		
			⅔ c	5⅓ fl oz	10⅔ Tbsp		
			⅝ c	5 fl oz	10 Tbsp		
			½ c	4 fl oz	8 Tbsp		
			⅜ c	3 fl oz	6 Tbsp		
			⅓ c	2⅔ fl oz	5⅓ Tbsp	16 tsp	
			¼ c	2 fl oz	4 Tbsp	12 tsp	
			⅛ c	1 fl oz	2 Tbsp	6 tsp	
				½ fl oz	1 Tbsp	3 tsp	
					½ Tbsp	1½ tsp	
						1 tsp	60 drops
						½ tsp	30 drops

U.S. TO METRIC CONVERSIONS

The conversions shown here are approximations. For more-precise conversions, use the formulas to the right.

VOLUME			WEIGHT			TEMPERATURE			CONVERSION FORMULAS
1 tsp	=	5 mL	1 oz	=	28 g	475°F	=	246°C	tsp × 4.929 = mL
1 Tbsp	=	15 mL	¼ lb (4 oz)	=	113 g	450°F	=	232°C	Tbsp × 14.787 = mL
1 fl oz	=	30 mL	½ lb (8 oz)	=	227 g	425°F	=	218°C	fl oz × 29.574 = mL
¼ c	=	59 mL	¾ lb (12 oz)	=	340 g	400°F	=	204°C	c × 236.588 = mL
½ c	=	118 mL	1 lb (16 oz)	=	½ kg	375°F	=	191°C	pt × 0.473 = L
¾ c	=	177 mL				350°F	=	177°C	qt × 0.946 = L
1 c	=	237 mL	**LENGTH**			325°F	=	163°C	oz × 28.35 = g
1 pt	=	½ L	1 in	=	2.5 cm	300°F	=	149°C	lb × 0.453 = kg
1 qt	=	1 L	5 in	=	12.7 cm	275°F	=	135°C	in × 2.54 = cm
1 gal	=	4.4 L	9 in	=	23 cm	250°F	=	121°C	(°F − 32) × 0.556 = °C

More books from
FOOD & WINE

Perfect Pairings

With chapters arranged by the most popular grape varieties, this collection of classic recipes takes the guesswork out of what dish to serve with your favorite wines. The easy-to-follow wine primers break down the nuances of grape varieties and regions so you can shop for bottles like a pro.

Master Recipes

An intrepid cook's guide to dishes you've only ever dreamed about making at home, this must-have manual breaks down the best way to DIY everything from beef jerky to babka. With step-by-step instructions and photos, experts share their foolproof methods for over 180 delicious dishes. Along the way, you'll learn indispensable skills like fermenting pickles, making bread, and tempering chocolate.

Mad Genius Tips

Did you know that you can poach a dozen eggs in a muffin tin? Or grate ginger with a fork? Or ripen bananas in the oven? Discover clever shortcuts and unexpected uses for everyday tools in a book that's as helpful as it is entertaining. Justin Chapple, the star of FOOD & WINE's *Mad Genius Tips* video series, shares more than 90 hacks for 100+ easy, fun, and delicious recipes.

TO ORDER, CALL 800-284-4145 OR VISIT **FOODANDWINE.COM/BOOKS**